Can Governments Earn Our Trust?

Donald F. Kettl

———————

Can Governments Earn Our Trust?

polity

First published in 2017 by Polity Press
Reprinted 2017, 2018 (twice)

Polity Press
65 Bridge Street
Cambridge CB2 1UR, UK

Polity Press
350 Main Street
Malden, MA 02148, USA

ISBN-13: 978-1-5095-2245-3
ISBN-13: 978-1-5095-2246-0 (paperback)

A catalog record for this book is available from the British Library.

Typeset in 11 on 15 pt Sabon
by Toppan Best-set Premedia Limited
Printed and bound in the United States by LSC Communications.

The publisher has used its best endeavors to ensure that the URLs for external websites referred to in this book are correct and active at the time of going to press. However, the publisher has no responsibility for the websites and can make no guarantee that a site will remain live or that the content is or will remain appropriate.

Every effort has been made to trace all copyright holders, but if any have been inadvertently overlooked the publisher will be pleased to include any necessary credits in any subsequent reprint or edition.

For further information on Polity, visit our website: politybooks.com

Contents

Figures and Table

Figures

Figures and Table

Table

Acknowledgments

An author wrestling with a puzzle as complex and long-lasting as trust in government requires a great deal of help. The basic issues go back a very long way; newer problems spill out daily. Pulling them all together into a single, short book is a daunting task. I want to thank Polity's editor, Louise Knight, who first inspired me to tackle this topic. Her insights into the things most worth doing were truly invaluable, and her enthusiastic support along the way has been inspiring. Nekane Tanaka Galdos, assistant editor at Polity, provided wonderful support at every step on the way. I'm also deeply appreciative of Leigh Mueller, whose keen skill as a copy-editor unquestionably made the book sharper and clearer.

In refining the book's arguments, I'm indebted to the reviewers for Polity, who were especially careful

Acknowledgments

in their reading and particularly helpful in their recommendations. Let me give my special thanks to Matthew Wright of American University and Jack Citrin at the University of California, Berkeley.

In addition, a greatly valued colleague, John DiIulio of the University of Pennsylvania, provided invaluable suggestions for improving the manuscript.

Finally, I want to thank my wife, Sue, whose own insights into the values that last have been an inspiration to me for the many years I've been lucky enough to have her as my spouse.

1

The Puzzle of Trust

The rising tide of distrust in government is surely one of the biggest challenges facing the world's democracies in the twenty-first century. The center of the problem is the United States, where trust in public institutions has dropped precipitously since the 1960s. In fact, according to public opinion surveys, Congress is less popular than head lice, cockroaches, traffic jams, and colonoscopies. But the problem is not just an American one. Edelman, a major global research firm, has surveyed 28 countries – and found that more than half of the public in more than half of the countries distrust their governments. The US, in fact, is about in the middle. Major democracies like Germany, Britain, Sweden, and Japan rank even lower.[1]

Can Governments Earn Our Trust?

Distrust in government often seems a largely US-centered problem, but its reach stretches much farther. Moreover, although distrust in government often seems a relatively recent problem, we will see in this book that it is an eternal, universal, and inescapable problem, not bound by time or place. At the same time, however, distrust is bad and getting worse. It is spreading, fueled by shock waves of populism. And it poses large, important challenges to the world's major democracies that demand attention.

That, in turn, frames the basic puzzle for this book. If distrust is inevitable but getting worse, if it has deep roots in the US but is spilling into other countries as well, is there anything that we – especially the officials we elect to lead us – can do about it? Can they *earn our trust?*

The basic patterns are clear. In the 28 nations that Edelman surveys, citizens trust nongovernmental organizations (NGOs) more than businesses, businesses more than the media, and the media more than government (see figure 1.1). Since government is the one institution whose leaders we collectively choose, and the one institution we count on to work on behalf of all of us, the rising tide of distrust is especially worrisome. Can we take action, by all of us for all of us?

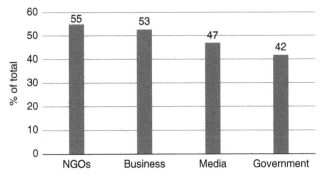

Figure 1.1 Trust in institutions
Source: 2016 Edelman Trust Barometer, "Executive Summary" (2016), www.edelman.com/insights/intellectual-property/2016-edelman-trust-barometer/executive-summary.

If distrust splinters our capacity to work together, the prospects for the survival of democracy are bleak.

But this book does not have a gloomy conclusion. The prospects for earning trust are, in fact, quite good – if we have the wits to discover and use the strategies that will help us to do so. After exploring how we got into this fix, we will examine how democratic government can in fact earn trust – and, in the process, at least modestly help to restore our confidence in its ability to govern us.

Trends in trust

"Trust" is a deceptively complex phenomenon, so definitions are important. In the political setting, trust occurs when citizens look at how their governments operate and conclude that their political leaders will keep their promises in a just, honest, and efficient way.[2]

But trust operates in two dimensions. *Social trust* describes the relationships among individuals, leading them to have confidence in their interactions with each other and, therefore, to cooperate in seeking common ground. Social trust thus supports governmental institutions, because individuals who trust each other are more likely to trust the decisions their governments make on their behalf. *Political trust* reflects the direct relationship between citizens and their governments. Trust in political institutions is a reflection of the confidence that individuals have that government does what they want and expect. The two dimensions of trust, of course, are closely related. But it is the erosion of political trust that is most worrisome for democratic institutions. Social trust captures the complicated relationships between individuals and how these interconnections spill over into institutions.[3] Political trust captures the struggles in the basic democratic relationship, between voters and governing institutions. Problems in political trust create much more direct worries about democracy's ability to govern. In this book, I will focus most on political trust, as we seek to understand the answers to important puzzles. What are the trends in political trust? Does it matter? And what can we do about it?

That puzzle, in turn, leads to a series of propositions about political trust, derived from the rich public opinion polling. They chart the rising tide of distrust.

Distrust in government is increasing – but not everywhere

The touchstone for analyses of distrust in government is the collection of American polls by Gallup and the Pew Research Center (see figure 1.2). The story is truly dismal, with a drop from the poll's high point in 1964, when 77 percent of Americans trusted government always or most of the time, to 2015, when the number plummeted to 19 percent.

% who trust the govt. in Washington always or most of the time

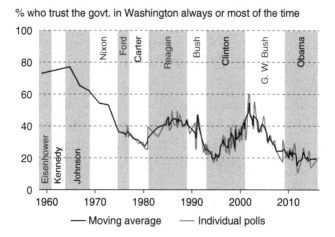

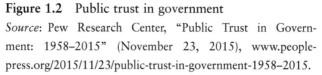

Figure 1.2 Public trust in government
Source: Pew Research Center, "Public Trust in Government: 1958–2015" (November 23, 2015), www.people-press.org/2015/11/23/public-trust-in-government-1958–2015.

But international comparisons are fascinating. The US is about average in distrust among Organization for Economic Co-operation and Development (OECD) countries, the world's leading democracies. In some countries – Switzerland, India, and Norway, for example – confidence in the national government is twice as high as in the US. In others – Spain, Greece, and Slovenia – it's only half as much (see figure 1.3). Moreover, in some countries

6

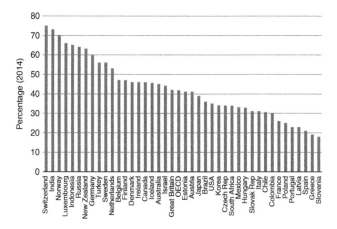

Figure 1.3 Confidence in national government
Source: OECD, *Government at a Glance: 2015*, fig. 11.1.

– including Spain, Finland, Slovenia, and South Africa – confidence in government dropped sharply from 2007 to 2014. In others – Russia, Germany, Israel, and Iceland – it went up almost as much (see figure 1.4). The US is at the center of the trust-in-government debate. But it certainly has no monopoly on distrust.

Even though the discouraging American trends suggest otherwise, trust doesn't always grow. High-trust governments like Finland have seen their citizens' confidence weaken, and the public's trust in low-trust governments like Slovakia has surged.

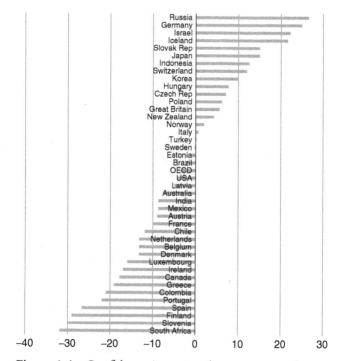

Figure 1.4 Confidence in national government: change from 2007 to 2014

Source: OECD, *Government at a Glance:* 2015, fig. 11.1.

Although distrust has risen over the long run, there are important variations in the trend, and they can be deceptively hard to disentangle. These disparities depend on the drivers of distrust, and we'll return to them in later chapters.

Distrust is greater at higher levels of government

Even though trust in the US federal government is dismal, trust and confidence in American state and local governments are much higher. In general, trust has been higher the lower the level of government. Trust in local governments was at 71 percent in 2016, and in state governments at 62 percent.[4] Moreover, trust in subnational governments has held relatively steady since the early 1970s, especially in comparison with the precipitous fall of trust in the federal government. In Europe, likewise, local governments tend to be trusted more than national ones.[5]

Trust is higher for the particular than for the general

Citizens can separate their trust in government in general from their trust in particular services that governments provide. The OECD, for example, found that 72 percent of citizens were satisfied with local police, 71 percent with health care, and 66 percent with the educational system, compared with just 40 percent with the national government.[6] In the US, polls have shown that citizens like most of what government does. A 2015 poll by the Pew Research Center, for example, found that a majority of citizens believed that government was doing a "very good" or "somewhat good" job on every function, except for helping people get out of poverty and managing the immigration system.[7] For the most part, they like what government does. It's government itself they can't stand.

This same finding carries over to political institutions. In a 2013 Gallup poll, 46 percent of Americans surveyed approved of the job their own member of Congress was doing – but just 16 percent approved of Congress overall. Only about a third of Americans, however, even knew the name of their member of Congress. Among those who did, approval was much higher, at 62 percent.[8] There's a simple message here: the closer the connection between citizens and the services they receive and those who represent them, the higher their trust. Citizens might not trust government much, but they trust more in what they know.

Not all citizens trust government equally

Edelman's surveys have found a huge trust gap between the informed public, which follows issues closely, and the mass public. Among members of the informed public, trust of NGOs, business, the media, and government was at 60 percent, compared with just 48 percent for the mass public. The surveys found that the gap was growing in 18 of 25 countries it surveyed, including France, Britain, the US, India, China, Brazil, and Germany. Moreover, the firm's surveys discovered a connection between income and trust. In the US, for example, 71 percent of upper-income individuals trusted institutions, compared with just 40 percent of lower-income individuals. Other countries had smaller but still-significant trust gaps linked to income inequality: France, Brazil, India, The Netherlands, Russia, and Britain.[9] Distrust is greatest among those earning the least.

Some good news about trust is bad news

In 2016, some poll-watchers celebrated a US Gallup survey that suggested the long slide in distrust might be easing. Confidence in Congress, the executive, and the judiciary all increased (even though it remained far below historical levels). But the good news hid an implicit warning. The improvements, analysts explained, were largely due to increased enthusiasm among Democrats, while Republicans' opinions hadn't budged: trust is increasingly partisan, and partisans tend to trust government more when their party is in power. That not only has important implications for *who* trusts government, since the balance of trust/distrust can easily flip with new elections. It also raises big concerns for the long-term patterns of distrust. The more partisans become polarized, the harder it is likely to be to restore trust in government among the public at large.[10]

No country can escape the challenge of distrust

China is a notable exception to these global trends, with 58 percent of respondents trusting their central government, according to a 2012 survey. Moreover, in the reverse of American trends, citizens trusted national government more than the city governments (although trust was 45 percent for the city governments). In 2010, the Pew Research Center found that 87 percent of the Chinese population was "satisfied with national conditions." The country's authoritarian government permits surprising levels of citizen autonomy, except in criticizing the party and its rule. The Communist party's governing philosophy builds on deeply rooted Confucian traditions about the importance of trust in authority.

However, even China's authoritarian government is increasingly struggling with problems of distrust. Trust in the party's government is lower among citizens who are younger, better educated, and more highly paid (and that, of course, is the reverse of the findings in Western democracies). As the Chinese economy develops, more citizens become more well-to-do, more citizens get better education, and younger citizens become the country's leaders, distrust is likely to grow. No country – even China with its authoritarian government – is immune to the challenges of trust in government.

Why does trust matter?

Distrust of institutions in general – and of government in particular – is high in many countries, and it threatens to deepen. If the problem is enduring and worsening, should we worry about it? What difference does trust in government make?

Can Governments Earn Our Trust?

Distrust affects political participation

Political scientists are sure that distrust in government affects political participation. They're just not sure how. Some theorists have argued that, as trust decreases, so too does political participation, especially through voting. After all, voter turnout in the US has declined as distrust has grown. Other theorists contend that higher distrust encourages groups to mobilize to affect political decisions. Anger at the process can lead activists to organize. In fact, there's evidence for both propositions, and the only sure conclusion is that the connection between distrust and political participation is very real but very complex. Which way distrust drives participation just isn't clear.[11]

Distrust can increase political polarization

It is clear, however, that strategies built on distrust can increase polarization. In the 1994 midterm congressional election in the United States, for example, Republican leader Newt Gingrich identified a list of labels that he suggested Republican candidates ought to use against their Democratic opponents: "corrupt," "red tape," "patronage," "pathetic," "sick," "abuse of power," "machine," "bosses," and "destructive."[12] It worked. His campaign produced the "Republican revolution," which led to Republican control of the US Senate and House of Representatives for the first time in 40 years. In 2016, Donald Trump proved even more successful in using distrust to build a coalition. Just 41 percent of Donald Trump's supporters had "a great deal of confidence" that votes across the country would be accurately counted, compared with 70 percent of Hillary Clinton's supporters.[13] Nearly half of Trump's supporters completely distrusted the economic data reported by the federal government, compared with just 5 percent of Clinton's supporters.[14] In each of these cases, higher distrust among key groups created a filter that, in turn, affected how they understood issues and the evidence supporting them, and that in turn increased polarization.

The same kind of polarization also fueled the United Kingdom's surprising Brexit vote in 2016, with 52 percent of Britons voting to Leave and 48 percent to Remain. Behind the vote was a profound gap in trust of business (67 percent versus 35 percent) and government (54 percent versus 26 percent) between the groups. As British journalist Anatole Kaletsky wrote before the vote, "the Brexit referendum is part of a global phenomenon, a populist revolt against established political parties, predominantly by older, poorer and less educated voters angry enough to tear down existing institutions and defy establishment politicians."[15] Two of the most surprising and most important votes of a generation both occurred in 2016 – Trump's victory in the US presidential race and Britain's decision to withdraw from the European Union. Both grew from polarization fed by distrust.

Distrust is expensive

In his 1995 classic on social trust, Francis Fukuyama argued that more distrust made it harder and more expensive to do anything. People who trust each other assume that individuals will keep their commitments. People who don't, on the other hand, need to invest enormous energy to set up rules, all of which have to be negotiated, sometimes litigated, and always enforced. Widespread distrust, he concluded, "imposes a kind of tax on all forms of activity, a tax that high-trust societies do not have to pay."[16] At the individual level, the higher the distrust, the more individuals have to bargain and battle over their disagreements. The more that's the case, the more governments need to define and manage the rules of the game. The more citizens distrust the government, the harder it is for government to set rules that stick. That, in turn, leads government to impose even more rules and to invest more energy to ensure compliance. The higher the levels of both social and political distrust, therefore, the higher the transaction costs for everything in society.

Distrust can increase noncompliance and corruption

Distrust reduces the willingness of individuals to comply with government regulations.[17] In most countries, for example, tax collections depend fundamentally on the voluntary compliance of citizens to report their income and pay the taxes due. Voluntary tax compliance in the US, the Internal Revenue Service estimates, is just over 80 percent. The one in five taxpayers who shirk their obligation, however, cost the Treasury $458 billion a year, almost as much as the federal government's entire budget deficit.[18] Moreover, noncompliance has grown, from 11.5 percent in 1984 to 18.3 percent in 2008–10.[19] There is no direct evidence that declining trust increased noncompliance, but, at the least, it is clear that higher distrust didn't help, and it's plausible that the less individuals trust the government in general – and tax collectors in particular – the less inclined they are likely to be to pay what the government says they owe. A 2015 survey found that just 31 percent of Americans trust the IRS to enforce the tax laws fairly.[20] Meanwhile, anti-tax slogans popular during the American revolution began appearing more often on car bumper stickers.

A team of Harvard researchers, moreover, found that in societies with high levels of trust, citizens expect low levels of regulation and corruption. On the other hand, more distrust increased the demand for rules, because citizens looked to the government to protect them from the abuses that arise in commerce. So, even though citizens might not trust the government or its regulations, they want more government rules because they don't trust each other.[21] And that, in turn, sets the stage for a depressing spiral. In low-trust societies, the increase in government regulations can lead to an increase in corruption, as citizens use bribes to cut through red tape.[22]

The Puzzle of Trust

Distrust can weaken support for redistribution

In a careful look at the connections between political trust and welfare policies, Marc Hetherington found that higher distrust in government led to lower support for programs that redistribute income. The argument goes like this. As distrust increases, citizens become increasingly suspicious of government programs that cost them more money but provide them with fewer benefits.[23] Citizens look carefully to see whether government works for them – and their support for government programs that benefit others, even the poor, diminishes. In fact, polls show that support for government programs dealing with the poor – helping people to get out of poverty – and that deal with the immigration system get the lowest support. These forces, moreover, spill over into the increasing partisan divide. Some of the biggest gaps between Democratic and Republican support for federal programs emerge in areas like access to health care and management of the economy, where there is also a difference between Republicans and Democrats in how well they think government works for them. The erosion of support for social welfare programs has spilled over into civil rights issues as well.

Can Governments Earn Our Trust?

Distrust can slow innovation

Distrust can also slow the pace of innovation, because lower trust can make individuals more cautious in making decisions about their futures – and the more cautious they are, the slower they are likely to be in adapting to the future.[24] Countries with higher overall levels of trust produced more eagerness to trust innovation.[25] Innovation depends vitally on trust: society's willingness to allow innovators to experiment, to demonstrate the value of their work without fear of retribution, and to reap the rewards of success. Innovation requires an instinct for experimentation, and that needs to build on an atmosphere of both social and political trust.

That can be very hard where distrust is high. In Flint, Michigan, a switch in the city's drinking water supply in 2014 led to contamination of the city's entire water system with lead. "Even now, the people of Flint, Mich., cannot trust what flows from their taps," a *Washington Post* reporter wrote 18 months later. The pastor of a Flint church said that the members of his congregation "are enraged, depressed, despondent, hopeless. You see the full gamut of emotions." When he visited the city in the Fall of 2016, President Barack Obama said, "you can't have a democracy where people feel like they don't count, where people feel like they're not heard."[26] Innovation depends on trust; distrust can undermine confidence in the government's work.

That can pose special problems in times of crisis, from natural disasters to terrorist attacks, when citizens count on government acting forcefully and effectively on their behalf. The sluggish response of President George W. Bush's administration to Hurricane Katrina's devastation of the American Gulf Coast in 2005 not only worsened the suffering caused by the storm. It led to a collapse of his popularity ratings from which he never recovered, and which weakened his ability to govern in the rest of his term.[27] The Japanese government's struggles to respond to a triple disaster in 2011 – an earthquake, tsunami, and nuclear meltdown – severely damaged the trust of citizens in the government.[28]

Distrust weakens the legitimacy of political institutions

One of the most important worries about the rise of distrust is its erosion of the legitimacy of government.[29] The connection between trust and legitimacy is an ancient one, dating back to the ancient

Greeks and their development of the foundations of the state. Nothing stands as a stronger argument about the importance of trust in government than the worry that distrust will undermine citizens' acceptance of government's authority, of its decisions, and of the policies it creates. Declining legitimacy can lead to violence, as countless coups have shown, and to collapse of governments, as the fall of the Soviet Union demonstrates. The worries are not far-fetched. In 2016, for example, only 21 percent of Americans said that the federal government had the consent of the governed.[30] Fukuyama worried that decaying trust could produce an unhappy spiral that could, in turn, lead to "an outright system collapse."[31] Even if the result is not quite that apocalyptic, the implications of distrust for democratic institutions are serious indeed.

The imperative to earn trust

Most of our discussion so far has focused on how distrust can damage democracy. But are we stuck in a downward spiral? Given the decline of trust over the years, can government earn it back?

Earning trust can seem a daunting challenge. The key to meeting it begins by recognizing that trust

22

– and distrust – have their roots in the relationship between individuals. Earning trust begins by finding common ground. That's just the strategy that former Australian Prime Minister Gough Whitlam tried on a visit to Great Britain when he was invited to give a speech at an event hosted by the Lord Mayor of London. It promised to be a difficult evening. Whitlam had been a Labor prime minister who had established state-funded health care, free university education, and other programs that advanced the size and scope of government. His host, the Lord Mayor, was an arch conservative. But Whitlam also discovered that the Lord Mayor had a distinguished career as an oarsman during his university days. At the black-tie dinner, Whitlam arose for a toast. "Your Worship, my Lords, Ladies and Gentleman," he began, "I came here this evening thinking that His Worship and I have absolutely nothing in common, but now I find that we are united by one thing, because as you know, he is a distinguished oarsman and I am a politician and the thing that unites us is that we both look one way and go the other."[32] The line got a big laugh – and helped build a connection between very different people.

That was a challenge that Hillary Clinton never solved during the 2016 presidential campaign. She found herself under attack for telling one of her audiences that "you need both a public and a private position" during contentious issues.[33] On one level, of course, that is inescapably true. No politician could survive long by telling the public exactly what she thought at all times. Successful deal-making always requires a deft hand at backroom negotiations. But, in the end, the relationship between citizens and their government has to be – and must be seen to be – genuine. Clinton never escaped the suspicion of many voters that her campaign was fundamentally opportunistic – that is, essentially untrustworthy. There were many reasons why she lost the tough and nasty race, but a bedrock reason was that she failed to earn voters' trust.

So that frames the central puzzle. Can government leaders – and government as a whole – earn our trust? To cut to the chase, the answer is yes. But that requires a careful understanding of the roots of distrust, how government can earn trust, and what roadblocks they need to navigate to make it stick.

2

The Case for Distrust

We talk about distrust as if it were a bad thing. Of course, as we saw in the first chapter, it brings danger to democracy, not least because it undermines its very legitimacy. But is distrust *always* a bad thing? The answer to this question is no. More fundamentally, is it an inevitable and persistent feature of the relationship between citizens and their government? Here the answer is yes. Government is impossible without the exercise of its power over citizens, and citizens have always been distrustful of how governments use that power. A certain measure of distrust thus is both inevitable, because no one likes having power exercised over them, and necessary, because distrust helps keep that power in check. But too much distrust can make it hard for government to do what citizens need, want, and expect. The challenge is balancing this inevitable distrust, in the exercise of power, with the necessity of trust, to allow government to work. That challenge has deep roots in history.

Consider the case of Caesar and his decision to bring his army from the province of Gaul into Italy. The Roman historian Suetonius reports he announced, "alea iacta est" in taking a force across a narrow river, the Rubicon, which separated Gaul from the seat of the empire. Since then, "crossing the Rubicon" and "the die is cast," the translation of his Latin utterance, have become the inescapable maxims for those making fateful and irreversible decisions – not only in the past but stretching into the future. Writers on *Star Trek: Deep Space Nine* borrowed from Caesar to title a 1995 episode, "The Die Is Cast." So did the writers of a Japanese anime television series in 2011. The Rubicon has become the stuff of legends, although the French put it differently: "les carrottes sont cuites" – "the carrots are cooked," a clever recognition that rivers can be uncrossed but carrots cannot be uncooked.

Caesar's decision was important because it cut to the core of how Romans viewed trust. The Romans were eager to expand their empire and empowered generals like Caesar to lead their legions across much of the known world. Generals like Caesar operated under *imperium*, a grant of power to conquer and rule. But *imperium* ended at the borders of Italy. Powerful generals backed by big armies might prove hard to stop, and Roman law forbade generals from bringing their soldiers into Italy. Caesar's bold crossing of the Rubicon with one of his legions not only was a statement of his power. Pompey, who was then consul, and much of the Senate saw Caesar's move as a direct challenge to the legitimacy of elected power in Rome. Caesar won the civil war that followed and became dictator. It went very well for him until a fateful day on the Ides of March in 44 BC.

At the core of Caesar's story was the fundamental question of legitimacy: on what basis can and should rulers exercise power? *Imperium* was based on a positive principle – supporting the expansion of Roman rule by fundamentally distrusting the power of generals. They didn't trust their generals to restrain their ambitions, and that restriction worked until Caesar's river crossing. Caesar's ambition makes the fundamental case for distrust of government: at the core, distrust of the exercise of power is necessary to control the way power is used. Indeed, British writer Norman Douglas said, "Distrust of authority should be the first civic duty." Distrust, therefore, surely can be a bad thing – but it is also inevitable. In democracies, it is essential for protecting fundamental values. Finding the balance is the trick.

The fundamentals of trust

Democratic legitimacy hinges on individuals' wary acceptance of government's power. That, in turn, leads to several broader propositions about the role of trust in society and, especially, in government.

Distrust is eternal

Such tensions of trust date from the earliest days of society itself. The word "trust" (or a variant) appears 188 times in the King James version of the Bible, with "confidence" appearing another 39 times. "Trust" is mentioned 540 times in the Complete Jewish Bible, and 92 times in an English translation of the Quran.[1] Many of these passages call for believers to put their trust in the Almighty, in exchange for His love and protection.

The book of Exodus, for example, revolves around issues of trust (even though the word doesn't appear in the King James version of the book, but it does make four appearances in the Common

Jewish Bible). In anticipating Fukuyama's argument about transaction costs by several thousand years, Exodus (in the New American Standard Bible translation used by Catholics) says: "For every breach of trust, whether it is for ox, for donkey, for sheep, for clothing, or for any lost thing about which one says, 'This is it,' the case of both parties shall come before the judges; he whom the judges condemn shall pay double to his neighbor" (22:9). Breaches of trust tear at the social fabric, and those who break that trust must compensate their neighbors.

The decision of the Israelites to leave Egypt, follow Moses, and journey into a new land required an enormous amount of trust in Yahweh. Much of this book of the Bible is full of symbols of trust, including crossing the Red Sea between walls of water that could easily have swallowed them up (and which, in the narrative, did just that to Pharaoh's army) and battling the Amalekites (when Moses needed help from Aaron and Hur to hold up his arms and bring the Lord's help for the Israelites' army). In both cases, Moses trusted Yahweh to provide the help needed. But his trust sometimes proved weak. When it came time for the Israelites to enter the promised land, Moses wasn't allowed to go with them, because he hadn't trusted the Lord to provide water to the people.

Can Governments Earn Our Trust?

Those who believe in sacred scriptures, from all religions, know that trust is the foundation of the Almighty's promises. Those who do not can nevertheless read in the scriptures a vast and powerful stream of social constructs based on how individuals trust (and sometimes don't) higher authorities, as well as each other. Important relationships build on trust, and always have. On the other hand, distrust can powerfully erode relationships.

Distrust inevitably flows
from the exercise of power

As Caesar's tale illustrates, power and distrust have always been linked. Humans distrust those who exercise power, because they are not confident that the powerful will be fair. "Fairness," moreover, is often in the eyes of the beholder, often viewed very personally, in terms of "how does the exercise of power affect me?" In the Bible's New Testament, Jesus called Matthew, a tax collector, to be one of his disciples. It wasn't a popular move, because local citizens distrusted tax collectors as the very embodiment of Roman power: "And when the Pharisees saw it, they said unto his disciples, Why eateth your Master with publicans and sinners?"[2]

Elsewhere in the New Testament, Luke reports that onlookers admonished Jesus for daring to eat with Zacchaeus, a rich chief tax collector.[3] In fact, the King James version has 25 mentions of "tax collector," all in unflattering terms – except in the cases that tax collectors surrendered their connection with the state in pursuit of religious virtue. The enduring message is that government power requires taxes and the collection of taxes creates distrust. Why would a good person, let alone someone trying to change the world, want to have dinner with an untrustworthy person who was exercising power on behalf of an occupying empire?

That point, of course, is not very different from the point made by the barons to King John at Runnymede in 1215, or by the founders of the United States when they declared independence from King George III in 1776. The barons didn't trust King John's exercise of power and forced him to sign a document guaranteeing them protection against imprisonment without cause, a fair system of justice, and limits on the king's ability to collect taxes from the barons. The Magna Carta is a remarkable document, perhaps most for the recognition of how the king's power challenged the barons and for the king's agreement to restrict his power to preserve it – and the remarkable skill of the monks who managed to produce such an important document in such a tiny scrawl on a single sheet of sheepskin.

More than 500 years later, the American colonists charged King George with a long list of offenses, which combined into "repeated injuries and usurpations" of the rights of Americans. It was such a fundamental violation of the rights of the colonists and of their proper relationship with the king that it led a congress of their leaders, meeting in Philadelphia, to declare "That these united Colonies are, and of Right ought to be Free and Independent States." It took a long and bitter war to win the point, but in the end the British king yet again found himself needing to accept limits on his power.

In time, Americans reconnected with trustworthiness, in the spirit of godliness. The American Civil War of the 1860s was not only a time of fundamental redefinition of the power of the national government over the states. It was a time of great religious fervor, which sought to connect the idea of a "perpetual union" with "God, liberty, and law," as a Pennsylvania minister wrote in a letter to Secretary of the Treasury Salmon P. Chase. Chase was persuaded by such entreaties, and in 1861 he wrote to his director of the mint, "No nation can be strong except in the strength of God, or safe except in His defense. The trust of our people in God should be declared on our national coins." That led to a decision in 1864, passed by Congress, to embrace the slogan, "In God We Trust," which first appeared on a 2-cent coin that year. Use of the slogan was intermittent, but since 1938 the motto has been on all US coins. In 1956, at the height of the Cold War, Congress adopted it as the official motto of the US, and it has appeared on all US currency since.[4]

On one level, the connections between God and trust are self-evident. In times of great stress, Americans have often sought divine protection as an umbrella of security and a source of guidance. This compares with the British, who have enshrined a request for God to save the king or queen in the national anthem, with deeper roots connecting the deity with the monarch reaching back a thousand years. It's an appeal to the Almighty to provide guidance to the sovereign in the exercise of power. But it's also a deep recognition that the exercise of great power requires strong guidance, that the Almighty's words can provide strong direction, and that such guidance can help provide a foundation for trust.

Can Governments Earn Our Trust?

Trust builds on legitimacy – and legitimacy depends on consent

Few nations have shared the American official embrace of the Almighty. Even in the US, the motto leads to a joke captured in Jean Shepherd's book: *In God We Trust: All Others Pay Cash.*[5] The underlying question is this: if the exercise of power generates distrust, on what basis can governments exercise power and be seen as trustworthy by their citizens?

For centuries, kings asserted a divine right to their kingship. That's the origin, in fact, of the inscription "dieu et mon droit," a French phrase adopted by English kings since Henry V. The assertion of divine right proved a handy way of asserting legitimacy – contesting the king meant picking a fight with God, and few of the king's opponents would want to risk their eternal souls in a dispute. The Enlightenment period gradually wrung most of the religious elements from the king's assertion of power, which became dangerous for religions, since kings might feel they had the right to dictate dogma, as Henry VIII's entanglements demonstrated. And it became dangerous for kings, since their people were becoming increasingly restive in societies where they argued that the king's power trampled on their rights as citizens.

That conflict reached a sharp focus when Americans met in Philadelphia in 1776 to debate independence from George III. They built heavily on principles set by Enlightenment philosophers, especially England's John Locke. For government's exercise of power to be legitimate, he argued in his *Second Treatise on Civil Government*, that power should be limited, based on the people's consent, and not exercised in violation of the people's fundamental rights. Power is governed by a social contract, Locke explained: "The liberty of man, in society, is to be under no other legislative power, but that established, by consent, in the commonwealth; nor under the dominion of any will, or restraint of any law, but what that legislative shall enact, according to the trust put in it."[6] Individuals unite in societies, Locke explained, to overcome the problems that come from the basic "state of nature." To protect their society and their property, they agree to rules, set by legislative power: "with this trust, that they shall be governed by declared laws, or else their peace, quiet, and property will still be at the same uncertainty, as it was in the state of nature."[7] Ultimately, it is the people who judge when the individual who exercises power "fails in his trust."[8]

Can Governments Earn Our Trust?

So, if distrust is inherent in the exercise of power, it's possible to build trust by constructing governing institutions to constrain its use – and to help the people hold the exercise of power accountable. No longer can any leader assert legitimacy on the basis of personal characteristics or by channeling the voice of the deity. Some try to govern by force of arms, but they can rule only as long as their power can squash dissent. For democratic governments, rule depends on legitimacy and legitimacy depends on the consent of the governed.

Trust depends on trustworthy institutions

Locke's prescription has heavily shaped the development of democratic institutions around the world. It has also laid the foundation for the people's trust in those institutions. If power rests in the people's hands, they delegate that power to government to act on their behalf. But they expect that government will in fact exercise power in ways that do not fail this trust, and they construct institutions of governance to ensure that governments keep the trust. It is in the administration of policy where the biggest dangers of abuse lie, and it is in policy implementation that the focus on trust is sharpest.

The central puzzle is how to balance the creation of power, so government can fulfill citizens' expectations, with the need to constrain it, so government's exercise of power doesn't abuse citizens. Government is effective when it can get the job done; citizens otherwise can have no confidence in the power government exercises on their behalf. It is trustworthy when it exercises that power in ways that generate results, prevent abuse of rights, and act in accord with citizens' wishes. Governments do this through institutions: legislative, executive, and judicial, in American-styled systems, and variants elsewhere in the rest of the world. Trust and confidence in government thus depend on the trustworthiness of its institutions.

It is in legislatures that the deepest problems of trust in government have developed. In the United States, the profound paradox is that Congress is the national institution most closely connected to the people, but it earns the lowest level of confidence, just 9 percent in 2016. That marks a 70 percent reduction from the level in 1991, a much bigger drop than for the presidency or the Supreme Court (see table 2.1). In democracies across much of the world, moreover, there is widespread distrust of national parliaments (see figure 2.1). But there is also wide variation in the level of trust over time

Table 2.1 Confidence in American national institutions

	"A great deal" or "quite a lot" of confidence – %			
	1991 Feb. 28–Mar. 3	2006 June 1–4	2016 June 1–5	Change: 1991–2016
Congress	30	19	9	−70.0%
Presidency	72	33	35	−51.4%
Supreme Court	48	40	36	−25.0%

Source: Gallup, "Confidence in institutions" (2016), www.gallup.com/poll/1597/confidence-institutions.aspx.

and across nations. In some countries, trust in national parliaments has grown substantially (see figure 2.2).

This underlines an important theme. Distrust is not an inescapable element of modern governance. Trust is a very dynamic concept, and it can shift substantially over time. It also varies greatly by country, with Americans particularly obsessed – and distressed – by distrust of government. But even in the US, distrust is not necessarily a troubling and inescapable problem.

The Case for Distrust

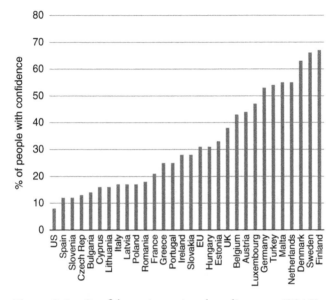

Figure 2.1 Confidence in national parliaments (2015)

Source: European Commission, Eurobarometer 83 (2015), http://ec.europa.eu/public_opinion/archives/eb/eb83/eb83_anx_en.pdf; and Gallup, "Confidence in institutions" (2016), www.gallup.com/poll/1597/confidence-institutions.aspx.

Trust is both cause and effect

Citizens' trust in their governments depends on the trustworthiness of their institutions. That trustworthiness, in turn, is both cause and effect. Trust begins with citizens' confidence, based on their previous

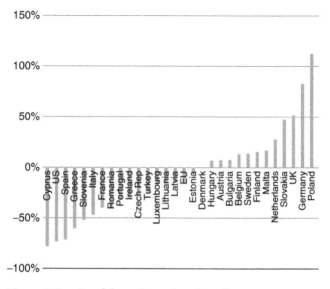

Figure 2.2 Confidence in national parliaments: percentage change, 2004–2015

Source: European Commission, Eurobarometer 83 (2015), http://ec.europa.eu/public_opinion/archives/eb/eb83/eb83_anx_en.pdf; European Commission, Eurobarometer 63 (2005), http://ec.europa.eu/public_opinion/archives/eb/eb63/eb63_en.pdf; and Gallup, "Confidence in institutions" (2016), www.gallup.com/poll/1597/confidence-institutions.aspx.

experiences, that government will do a good job in performing its basic duties, like ensuring security, stability, opportunity, fair treatment, and economic prosperity. The level of trust, in turn, frames citizens' expectations about how well political leaders and their political institutions will perform.[9] Trust thus flows from citizens' experiences. Citizens who feel insecure or who have been disappointed by their interactions with government will have lower levels of trust. Lower levels of trust, in turn, shape citizens' views about their institutions, and their expectations about how well government will perform or step up to new challenges.

Trust thus depends on the past and shapes the future. In social science terms, it is both an independent and dependent variable: a force that shapes expectations and that is the product of past experiences. This matters for two reasons. First, it only begins to hint at the complex forces shaping trust and the effects that distrust have on the political system. Second, it raises enormous challenges in determining whether – and how – government can earn trust. It's easy to begin with a discouraging proposition: the more distrust is the product of past performance, the harder it will be to dislodge it. Fortunately, as we shall see, there are hopeful roads forward.

Tides of distrust, cycles of reform

We tend to see distrust of government as a relatively modern phenomenon, which especially plagues the

US and some other major democracies. As we have seen, however, issues of trust have been part of the human condition as long as humans have interacted with each other. The story of humankind in the Bible only makes it to chapter 3 of Genesis before a fundamental problem of trust arises: Adam explains he ate of the forbidden fruit because Eve gave it to him. Distrust is an inevitable counterpart of the exercise of governmental power, as Caesar's tale makes clear. Moreover, a measure of distrust can be a healthy check on government itself. Too much power can be intoxicating and can lead to abuse; a distrust of how leaders exercise power has always been an important means of holding leaders accountable.

The baseline of political trust

But first, there is an important question: if distrust is eternal, why does it seem such an urgent, new phenomenon? Part of the explanation comes from the rise of polling in the 1950s. In the immediate post-World War II years, the social sciences became increasingly focused on honing statistical techniques. Survey research helped lead the charge, with the rise of improved means of sampling the opinions of citizens and processing them with high-speed computers. George Gallup laid the foundation, beginning in 1936, to develop polling as a tool for marketing. The National Opinion Research Center was established in 1941 and, in 1947, the American Association for Public Opinion Research and the World Association for Public Opinion Research were founded. Researchers like Elmo Roper, Paul F. Lazarsfeld, Angus Campbell, and Harold D. Lasswell vastly improved polling techniques, and candidates like American President Dwight D. Eisenhower found the tool extremely helpful in shaping their campaigns.

The American National Election Study began surveying Americans about their trust in government in 1958 and found that 73 percent of those surveyed had "trust in the government in Washington always or most of the time." The number edged up to 76 percent in 1964, just before Lyndon B. Johnson's landslide presidential victory. It then began its steady drop to just 25 percent in 1980, a level from which it has never recovered for long.[10] The late 1950s was an especially important – but perhaps atypical – benchmark from which to measure trust. Americans were relatively content. The economy was booming, with growth of more than 5 percent in 1958. Americans were building new high-speed highways on which to drive bigger, faster cars from new suburbs to new vacation spots like Disneyland. Not everything was rosy, of course. The Cold War was a hot problem, and when the Soviet Union launched its first satellite into orbit in 1957, the space race fueled tremendous anxiety about new threats to national security. But, as so often has happened in polling, external threats tended to boost citizens' support for their government's efforts to deal with them.

Some of the trust anxiety, therefore, surely flows from the fact that the baseline comes from a snapshot in time when trust in government was probably about as high as it's ever been. That, in turn, is a historical artifact of a time when sophisticated polling of the public burst onto the scene and when Americans were feeling good about their government – and about the need for it to work well. Trust in the American government has since been plagued by a stream of crises – Vietnam and Watergate, political scandals, and economic recessions, particularly the Great Recession of the late 2000s – that all tended to drive trust down. At the same time, gridlock grew and public confidence in government's ability to work shrank.

And some of the trust anxiety comes from declining trust in virtually all institutions. In the US for example, confidence in a basket of major institutions has fallen below historical averages. In a 2016 snapshot, Gallup found wide variation for confidence in American institutions, with very high confidence in the military, small business, and the police, and far lower confidence in television news, newspapers, and big business, with Congress, not surprisingly, bringing up the rear (see figure 2.3).

Trust can sometimes rise

Distrust thus is inevitably a constant phenomenon, since it grows from human interactions – especially in the strategies to transfer great power to governments to act on citizens' behalf. But just as human interactions change, so too does distrust. Moreover, it does not always slide inexorably downward and hamstring governmental action.

In America during the late nineteenth and early twentieth centuries, for example, public distrust toward big business and corporate trusts bubbled over. Unregulated free markets had fueled an impressive industrial movement, but they also led to monopoly power that enriched owners, and abusive conditions that plagued workers. Republicans and Democrats – and rogue organizers in the short-lived

June 1–5, 2016

■ % Great deal   ■ % Quite a lot

Institution	% Great deal	% Quite a lot
The military	41	32
Small business	30	38
The police	25	31
The church or organized religion	20	21
The medical system	17	22
The presidency	16	20
The U.S. Supreme Court	15	21
Government schools	14	16
Banks	11	16
Organized labor	8	15
The criminal justice system	9	14
Television news	8	13
Newspapers	8	12
Big business	6	12
Congress		6

Figure 2.3   Confidence in American institutions
Source: Gallup, "Confidence in institutions" (2016), www .gallup.com/poll/1597/confidence-institutions.aspx.

Progressive party – led a dramatic movement to increase government's power and bring corporate power under stronger control. This Progressive movement came, of course, long before public opinion polls could tell us how much distrust there was toward either big business or big government. But the evidence is plain: elected officials led an aggressive campaign to create new government agencies like the Food and Drug Administration and the departments of Labor and Commerce to increase government's power, and those who led the campaign got themselves re-elected. There's no better sign of trust in their work.

In Great Britain, there was a similar movement, which led to reforms in the Poor Laws, regulations on the use of children as chimney sweeps, and protections for factory workers and coal miners. There was an aggressive expansion of taxpayer-funded local schools, first through primary education and then with secondary schools. New laws expanded government protection of water and improvement of slums. Government stepped in to improve sewage and housing. In fact, the institution of football in England owes much to the reform movement. Workers won shorter working hours on weekends, and organized football sprang up to fill the time. Similar movements spread through Germany, France, and other European nations. Insurance programs for old age and sickness began spreading. So, too, did the right to vote, although women's suffrage in many countries awaited the end of World War I.

Even a casual reading of history, moreover, suggests that trust in government has not always been at the heights the polls discovered in the late 1950s. Furthermore, while trust in many governments has spiraled downwards since the 1960s, trust in other governments has actually increased. Distrust isn't on an inexorably unhappy path, and the world's nations are not always in sync. Trust has risen and fallen over time, sometimes more in some nations than in others. So there's hope that trust will not always remain at the lows of the 2010s. In historical terms, trust doesn't necessarily spiral downward. Moreover, at least periodically, there has been sufficient trust in government to vastly increase its power.

Consider, for example, the American reaction to the 2001 terrorist attacks. According to a *CBS News / New York Times* poll, trust rose to 55 percent, a level not seen since 1970.[11] Reacting to the horror of that September morning, Americans rallied around their flag and their government. The George W. Bush administration built on that upswell of trust to launch major wars in Iraq and Afghanistan, to create a new Department of Homeland Security, and to pass a package of surveillance tools that allowed unprecedented probing of Americans' private lives. But it didn't last. Public support for the wars dwindled as they dragged on and when George W. Bush's "Mission Accomplished" claim rang hollow. Leaked documents from the National Security Agency showed that the government was intercepting information on a far higher scale than most Americans imagined. Public trust in government sank – to historically low levels, pushed even lower by the 2008 economic collapse.

Stuck in a rut

Trust and distrust run in cycles, but the evidence of the 1990s and 2000s suggests that the expansion of government power can plant the seeds of distrust of that power, which sprout sometimes immediately, sometimes years later. Some analysts, in fact, argue that it will be virtually impossible for trust to recover to the levels of the 1960s. Marc J. Hetherington and Thomas J. Rudolph argue that "low levels of political trust are here to stay."[12]

The case that we are stuck with distrust builds on four powerful – and discouraging – arguments. First, in the broad sweep of history, Western democracies are struggling with growing *clientelism*. As more interests have become better organized, they have gained more control over government decisions. Government tends to reflect their preferences, not the interests of citizens as a whole. Francis

Fukuyama argues that political decay – declining competence and rising distrust – is the result.[13]

Second, American democracy, in particular, has become increasingly plagued by *polarization*, fueled by political parties that cannot escape their extreme ideological bases. The parties – especially the Republicans – successfully redrew district boundaries to enhance their ability to win and keep seats. That, in turn, fueled gridlock and made it increasingly difficult for America's political institutions, especially Congress, to find a middle ground for passing legislation. As bad as the trend seemed, Thomas E. Mann and Norman J. Ornstein sadly argued, "it's even worse than it looks."[14]

Third, the rise of *social media and 24/7 news* has made the framework for the policy agenda ever more shaky. The flood of news outlets creates an insatiable demand for new stories to draw readers. The success of Facebook and Twitter has only reinforced that demand, fed by everything from piano-playing cats that entertain viewers to echo-chamber political debates that reinforce ideological prejudices. Issues can slide onto and off the national stage very quickly. How the public judges them can be shaped by information that might or might not track with strong evidence. Which issues matter most to people and how they view them, have thus become hyper-dynamic, and that in turn tends to "trigger changes in the criteria people use to evaluate government," Hetherington and Rudolph argue.[15] Since trust in government builds on those evaluations, it has become increasingly unstable as well.

Fourth, there is growing perception that government's *performance*, too often, is simply poor. Peter H. Schuck savages the performance of the US federal government, for example, and concludes that "the federal government does in fact perform poorly in a vast range of domestic programs."[16] That conclusion is the subject of fierce debate. But quite apart from the government's actual performance, which is hard to assess overall, it is impossible to escape the conclusion that most citizens *think* that government performs poorly. Americans, in fact, rate the federal government's performance at the bottom of all the sectors surveyed – lower than oil and gas, the legal field, health care, and pharmaceuticals.[17]

Understanding the case for distrust

Distrust carries enormous costs, as we saw in the last chapter. But distrust is inevitable with the government's use of power, and there can be no government without the exercise of power. The central problem of democracy is exercising that power while holding it accountable to the people, but in the last decades of the twentieth century there was a rising tide of distrust: growing concern that government's power served narrow interests, not the people as a whole. In fact, there is a powerful paradox: the very institutions designed to be the people's most powerful check on government, the legislature, are often the least trusted. That's surely the case for the American Congress, and similar problems have spilled over into other nations as well. The explanation is simple: citizens put their trust in their elected representatives to hold government's power in check, but they increasingly believe that government is drifting out of touch. Distrust rises. And that reinforces the argument that Hetherington and Rudolph made: we are stuck, and it's going to be hard to recover.

That, in turn, takes us back to the basic puzzle of this book: *can governments earn our trust?* There are two important propositions that build the foundation for thinking about solutions. First, distrust is inevitable in human relationships, because those relationships build on the exercise of power. Losers in the power game – or those who think they might lose – often deeply distrust the game itself. Those who win tend to worry about whether they'll be able to continue to do so. Distrust is baked deeply into the crust of social institutions in general and democratic ones in particular.

Second, at least *some* distrust is healthy. In preparing for negotiations with Soviet President Mikhail Gorbachev in 1986, President Ronald Reagan famously said "Trust – but verify." Reagan's constant use of the phrase annoyed Gorbachev, because it came from Russian ("doveryai no proveryai") and he disliked having the proverb turned against him.[18] But a measure of distrust – verifying what others promise – can be healthy in negotiations.

Indeed, managing distrust was central to the creation of the American republic in Philadelphia. Most Americans have forgotten that the country's Constitution is really America 2.0, a fresh governing scheme created when the original one failed. When the young nation declared independence, distrust of the king in particular and of power in general was so great that the founders could agree on only a loose confederation. That barely worked to win the revolution; it didn't work at all to govern the new country. So, in 1787, the founders met again in Philadelphia, this time to create a stronger government with a clear Constitution. But even then, distrust of concentrated power, especially executive power, remained so strong that the founders first created the Congress to hold the presidency in check. The consensus around the role of the executive was so uneasy that it drew Alexander Hamilton, who had served as secretary of the treasury, into a duel with Aaron Burr, the nation's vice president. They fought over executive power, among many other things. It cost Hamilton his life – and the high drama centuries later became a surprising mega-hit as a Broadway musical.

In measured doses, distrust is an essential building block of democratic government. Building trust, on the other hand, is *the* essential building block for the legitimacy of democratic government. Trust and distrust, therefore, are not absolutes but counterbalances, but those balances are never steady or stable. Our worry is that the balance has tipped too far, especially in the US – that distrust has crippled democracy and pushed government's ability to perform to a crisis point.

3

Earning Trust

So far in this book, the story has been mostly disheartening: many citizens don't trust government, distrust is rooted in deep forces, and it might prove hard to dislodge. Perhaps the story is not quite so bleak, since trust in some countries is higher than in others. Distrust therefore is not an inescapable maelstrom trapping modern democracies. But American democracy, in particular, seems especially caught in hard-to-break snares, and escaping distrust is a particular problem for the world's largest democracy.

That frames the tough question: if a nation, a government, or a leader wants to increase trust, is there *anything* they can do? Can they earn trust?

Earning trust through transparency

The foundation for building trust begins with the argument for *transparency*. The central idea, developed during the Enlightenment, is that government's legitimacy builds on the consent of the governed. But, to give consent, citizens must know what government is doing and find effective levers of influence. James Madison, one of America's most distinguished founders, and later the country's fourth president, wrote in Federalist 51, part of a series of papers devoted to making the case for the new American Constitution: "If angels were to govern men, neither external nor internal controls on government would be necessary. In framing a government which is to be administered by men over men, the great difficulty lies in this: you must first enable the government to control the governed; and in the next place oblige it to control itself." Of course, men are not angels, so democracy requires ways of helping the governed to control government. That begins, in the minds of many theorists and citizens alike, with the most important and fundamental tool to build trust: transparency.

Analysts often strongly argue, "you can't have trust without transparency."[1] That idea has led reformers to campaign for forcing more government meetings to be open, for making it easier for citizens to gain access to records, and for bringing more sunshine to government's operations. The underlying assumption is that the more information that's available to the public, the more accountable and better-performing government will be. In the United States, the Sunlight Foundation is singularly devoted to making all government information open and available in real time. A global organization, Transparency International, seeks to bring greater openness to governments everywhere, through chapters in more than 100 countries. The Web Foundation has ranked the most transparent countries in the world, with the United Kingdom first, followed by the US, Sweden, and a tie between New Zealand and France. At the bottom of the 86 countries surveyed are Mali, Haiti, and Myanmar.[2]

The logic seems inescapable: citizens will place more trust in organizations whose behavior is more trustworthy – and whose trustworthiness they can readily see. But if the case for transparency seems self-evident, the reality is far more complex, for five reasons.

First, the pursuit of "transparency" often flows more from the pursuit of compliance with law than a commitment toward openness. Many governments have created new procedures, ranging from open records and open meetings to open data. Many government agencies end up scrambling to determine how best to comply with the law – and then to get their work done, as a separate proposition. That means they often separate the two streams instead of viewing transparency as how *all* work gets done. That, in turn, often frustrates citizens, who view transparency as a paper commitment with little real meaning.

Second, transparency often conflicts with other requirements. Agencies inevitably face the challenge of effectively delivering services, winning the political support of important stakeholders, and obtaining the resources they want in a tough environment in which other agencies are fighting in the same space for the same things. Transparency about problems in the past and strategies for the future can undermine, not help, in the rough battles that shape the political world. Feinting and indirection, trial balloons and bluster, are inevitable bits of the political landscape. No matter how devoted a government agency and its leaders might be in principle to transparent government, there are always fierce pressures fighting against full and open disclosure. Government agencies, in fact, are often tempted to be transparent when it helps them, to cover their tactics when openness seems dangerous, to some-times flood the field with more information than anyone could manage, and to focus narrowly on what they must do to comply with the law. What citizens might want isn't always what agencies provide. What information is released and what is not, in fact, are inevitably part of large political strategies.[3]

Third, more transparency can sometimes lead to less trust. A researcher conducted an experiment in Sweden, a high-trust country, and asked those sur-veyed whether they favored eliminating an *in vitro* fertilization program to channel more money for adolescent psychiatric services. Making the tradeoff explicit highlighted the underlying value conflicts in the decision, and that lowered trust in health care in general. In fact, those who had no information about the procedures involved had higher trust in the system. Sometimes, more information can produce less trust in government's decisions.[4]

Fourth, not all societies view trust equally. A research team set out to gauge the effect of more transparency on citizens' trust in The Netherlands and in South Korea through web-based experi-ments. Dutch subjects were surveyed on questions about air pollution; in South Korea, the respond-ents were asked about theft prevention. More trans-parency lowered trust in both countries about similar issues – but much more in South Korea than in The Netherlands. The Dutch tend to have a lower power distance between citizens and government officials and a shorter-term time horizon for exploring problems. South Koreans, for example, have a greater power distance and tend to take a longer-term view of issues because of the deep influence of Confucianism. The greater the power distance between citizens and their government and the more citizens take a long-term view, the less transparency improves trust, the researchers argued.[5]

Fifth, transparency can be scary, as the famous aphorism reminds us: "Laws are like sausages, it is better not to see them being made." Economist Justin Wolfers concluded that the vast movement toward greater transparency in government's operations in the last generation might also be fueling distrust of its operations. "We actually now get to see," he explained, "into that smoke-filled room where we're seeing the deals being cut." When "you see how sausage is made," Wolfers concluded, "you don't like eating sausage as much anymore." Thus, he said, it might be impossible to recover the levels of trust measured in the 1960s' surveys, precisely because much greater transparency makes it far easier to see government's many warts and blemishes, much more closely. "The political landscape and the technology with which we monitor our government [have] changed," he argued.[6]

Nothing captures the sausage-making analogy more than the recurring wars against "fraud, waste, and abuse" in government. In the US, this unholy trinity has become blurred as a single, blended phrase, which captures both the complexity of government's operations and a cynicism that they inherently don't work well. In Britain, there is a Serious Fraud Office – they don't spend time on just mundane fraud – charged with investigating "fraud, tricks and scams." The perception that fraud, waste, and abuse are an inevitable part of government tends, in turn, to feed the drumbeat of criticism about government and to undermine trust.[7] With 24/7 broadcasts to fill, the media have found tales of fraud an irresistible bait. Many reporters see themselves in the mold of Bob Woodward and Carl Bernstein, whose *Washington Post* investigations of Richard Nixon's abuse of power during the Watergate crisis in the early 1970s helped bring down his presidency. Whistleblowers like Edward Snowden, with his release of documents from deep inside America's National Security Agency, and Wiki-Leaks, which has distributed a vast supply of purloined papers, have kept that spirit alive. Shining a bright light of transparency into government's nooks and crannies has become a central strategy of reporters. With an unlimited Internet to fill and an ever more complex government providing endless tales of problems, transparency and distrust have become intertwined.[8]

There's no doubt that trust depends on transparency. But there's also no doubt that transparency is a complex concept, and that full disclosure can actually undermine trust. Transparency, in fact, is just as slippery and difficult an issue as trust itself.

Trust: wholesale and retail dimensions

Earning trust therefore requires a far more nuanced approach, one which builds on the fundamental relationship between people and their governments. For centuries, theorists have held that this relationship is a social contract, in which citizens support government in exchange for what government gives to them. In the nineteenth century, Walter Bagehot, the celebrated British essayist, broke that notion into two parts. He argued that the British Constitution depended on two elements: the "dignified" and the "efficient." The role of the dignified, he wrote, is to "excite and preserve the reverence of the population." In the British Constitution, that is the role of the monarch, but all democracies need a taste of dignity. The role of the efficient is to "employ that homage in the work of government." That is the role of the cabinet and the administrators it supervises, and all democracies – indeed, all governments – need that.[9] If citizens become unexcited and unreverential about government, if its dignity erodes, then its legitimacy crumbles. And if government loses the capacity to efficiently carry out its work, public support evaporates. Bagehot thus points to the central role of trust in securing the legitimacy of government, whether it has the blessings of monarchy or not.

That, in turn, sets the foundation for the two important elements of trust in government. Dignity operates at the *wholesale* level, where trust depends on creating confidence in the ability of government and its institutions, at the highest level, to represent its people and to perform fairly on their behalf. Efficiency operates at the *retail* level, where trust depends on creating confidence in government's ability to deliver on its policies, fairly and effectively, at the operational level where government connects directly with the people. Trust therefore is not a large, abstract, undifferentiated idea. Rather, it is a single term that captures a complex set of relationships between government and its citizens, relationships that operate on different levels and that, therefore, create a vast range of challenges.

Those challenges, in turn, create opportunities. Most of the polling and analysis about trust in government focuses on the level of system-based, wholesale interactions. Do citizens trust government, as a whole, or individual branches, like Congress? Those opinions are broad, built on interactions over time across a wide array of issues, and are therefore very hard to change. On the other hand, government does not operate just on this broad system level but, rather, on a vast array of individual interactions. It might just be possible to improve those retail-level interactions – to increase their efficiency, in Bagehot's formulation. And if that's possible, it might just be possible to earn trust. We'll come back to this proposition shortly. But first, let's look at the wholesale-level challenges that government faces, beginning with the relationship between wholesale-level trust and income inequality.

Wholesale trust and inequality

Earning trust at the wholesale level often depends on citizens' place in society and, in particular, whether they think society treats them fairly. In fact, trust hinges most fundamentally on income inequality. Indeed, it is in income inequality where the streams of social and political inequality come together: in the social trust realm, with research by Robert Putnam and Francis Fukuyama; and in the world of political trust, with work by Eric M. Uslaner, Mitchell Brown, Marc Hetherington, Thomas J. Rudolph, and many others.[10] It is the argument most often raised as the explanation for distrust.

In an unusually wide-ranging 2013 speech, President Barack Obama explored the issue. He said, "rising inequality and declining mobility are also bad for our families and social cohesion – not just because we tend to trust our institutions less, but studies show we actually tend to trust each other less when there's greater inequality." Obama continued, "people get the bad taste that the system is rigged, and that increases cynicism and polarization, and it decreases the political participation that is a requisite part of our system of self-government." In fact, he concluded, "rising inequality and declining mobility are bad for our democracy."[11]

Across the globe, trust in others is higher when income is more equally distributed. In the mid-2000s, OECD analysts compared citizens' sense of trust with the level of income inequality, measured by the Gini coefficient (where zero represents perfect income equality). The research is striking. Nations with the highest levels of income equality, like Denmark, Sweden, Norway, Finland, and The Netherlands, had the highest levels of trust. On the other hand, nations with higher inequality, like Mexico and Turkey, had lower levels of trust. The US, along with Poland, ranks relatively low in both trust and equality. Great Britain ranked a bit higher on both (see figure 3.1). Lower income inequality and higher trust in government were linked.

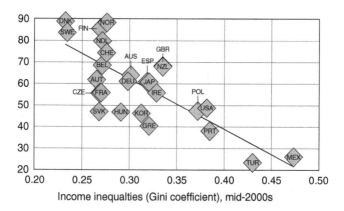

Figure 3.1 Social trust and income inequality: percentage of people expressing high trust in others

Source: OECD, *Society at a Glance 2011: OECD Social Indicators* (Paris: OECD, 2011), www.oecd-ilibrary.org/social-issues-migration-health/society-at-a-glance-2011_soc_glance-2011-en.

Moreover, researchers have found, trust varies among individuals. Men, in general, are more trusting than women, by a small margin. Younger individuals are less trusting than older people. The more education an individual receives, the higher the trust. And the poor tend to be less trusting than the more well-to-do (see figure 3.2). The consensus of researchers around these propositions, moreover, tends to be very strong.[12]

These findings raise three very interesting points. First, there are big variations in trust. Much of the analysis, which builds on the US case, tends to treat

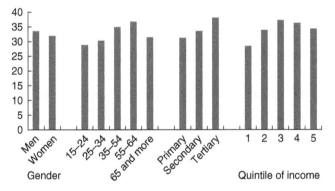

Figure 3.2 Trust in others by gender, age, education, and income

Source: OECD, *How's Life? Measuring Well-Being* (Paris: OECD, 2011), Figure 8.6.

trust as a big, depressing, spiraling phenomenon. But distrust is neither inevitable nor uniform. Understanding its causes and, more importantly, determining how to shift it is thus deceptively complex.

Second, income inequality and distrust are closely connected, but the data don't demonstrate what causes what. Does lower trust somehow produce more income inequality, perhaps because citizens don't trust their governments with the power to frame policies to address social and economic differences? Or does income inequality reduce trust, because those left behind don't trust the system to treat them fairly? The statistics show relationships, not causality.

Third, the latter explanation – that rising income inequality drives down trust – seems most plausible, but it is also very abstract. Just what can government officials do to reduce income inequality? Obama's 2013 speech laid out a very aggressive plan. He argued for stronger anti-discrimination laws, to protect opportunities for racial minorities and women; good pre-school programs for all children, better standard-based primary education, and more financial support for higher education; economic relief for those hurt by technological change; stronger collective bargaining; a higher minimum wage; more social welfare programs focused on workers hit hardest by the recession of the late 2000s; simplifying the tax code, especially for corporations; a trade agenda that grows exports; removal of outdated or ineffective government regulations; a more sensible budget that shrinks government deficits; better government programs to encourage savings for retirement; and stronger overall economic growth.

This is, of course, a very ambitious and sweeping agenda. It might help to drive growth and reduce income inequality. It's not clear that the agenda would, in fact, drive down distrust. But it is virtually certain that no president – indeed, no leader of any of the world's great democracies – would be able to drive this agenda far. It is big, complicated, expensive, and full of ideological assumptions that conservatives would fight at every turn. In fact, during the 2016 presidential election, Donald J. Trump argued that a combination of tax cuts, higher tariffs, and forced deportation of illegal immigrants would provide more opportunity for Americans. Political support for broad policy prescriptions of either ideological stripe is muddy, at best. And, in any event, few of the steps could be completed within any president's term of office – at least to the extent that the president could point to clear reductions in income inequality and take credit for having achieved them. Furthermore, no matter how successful any president might be in pushing big ideas forward, the increasingly interconnected global economy makes it hard for any country, even one as large as the US, to steer its own economic ship.

So if higher trust depends fundamentally on greater income inequality, if the connections between big policy changes and reductions in income inequality are hard to demonstrate, if the ability of any leader to marshal the political support to make sweeping changes to reduce income inequality is limited, and if the global marketplace makes it hard for any country to move forward on its own, then the ability of any elected official to improve wholesale trust seems a faint dream. That frames the fundamental paradox of wholesale trust: moving the needle on income inequality seems the strongest way to improve trust, but it is also the most elusive. Compounding the problem is a rising lack of confidence that government programs work anyway – and this rising distrust makes it hard to pursue programs that reduce income inequality. On this central issue, therefore, governments and their officials are set up to fail on wholesale trust, because they are being measured by yardsticks they can barely control. And, as we shall see in the next chapter, they are also facing rising challenges that Bagehot would recognize. The assault on the dignity of government has rarely been damaging.

Retail trust and the citizen experience

In Bagehot's terms, the other element of government's role is efficiency. Efficiency, in turn, builds on the *retail* activities of government: the interactions between citizens (as taxpayers) and government (as regulator of behavior and provider of services). As research on both the private and public sectors demonstrates, retail trust is something that elected government officials – and even individual government managers – can mend because every interaction offers an opportunity for improvement.

Private-sector analysts have focused especially on this strategy. Companies might advertise to define their *brand*, but customers concentrate most on their *experiences*. No amount of advertising can change the experience that customers have with products, so improving that experience is the best way to strengthen the brand – and increase profits. As Forrester, a leading global research and consulting firm, concluded, "customer expectations are growing at a lightning pace" and most companies are falling behind, even though they're investing much effort to catch up. What customers demand, Forrester found, were "easy, frictionless, and personalized experiences." The road to success, in turn, built on radically transforming how companies connected with customers on every transaction. Better customer experiences, in turn, produced bigger profits.[13]

How do government agencies stack up to these standards? Forrester's assessment of citizens' experiences with US federal government agencies is discouraging.[14] Its 2016 survey of 15 federal agencies found a customer experience lower than in any private-sector industry. The reason, Forrester said, was that "federal agencies don't focus on the right things," especially in improving citizens' interactions with government. Experience in dealing with the government agencies was three times more likely to be "very poor" or "poor" than with private companies. More than two-thirds of the organizations in the bottom 5 percent in the overall US customer experience index were federal agencies.

From this gloomy story, however, emerge some agencies that made substantial progress. For example, the Bureau of Consular Affairs in the State Department, the agency responsible for issuing passports, produced the second-biggest increase in customer experience scores of any organization, in government or out. It created a digital passport application form and launched live Twitter sessions to answer citizens' questions. The result was a score equal to a typical credit-card provider or retail bank. Two much-maligned federal operations, Healthcare.gov, the website for national health insurance that famously crashed at its launch in the Obama administration, and the Internal Revenue Service (IRS), the tax-collection agency, each improved their scores – more, in fact, than almost all private companies. Healthcare.gov improved its website to make it easier for citizens to shop for health insurance plans, estimate their costs, and examine which plans included which physicians and medications. The IRS created a mobile app, IRS2Go, which allowed taxpayers to check their bill and refund status, and to connect with the agency by social media or phone. Use of the app increased 30 percent in 2016 and taxpayers found it an easy way to get help with an unpopular task.

Performance and trust

Citizens' experiences with government rank lower than with any private industry, so it's easy to see why trust in government is low. But some government agencies do well and, perhaps most importantly, some government managers are making big progress. Here lies the foundation for earning trust. The US is not the only country struggling with the problem of trust, and some of the most interesting improvements have come from some of the most surprising places.

Earning retail trust through performance

In 2007, for example, the governor of Brazil's state of Pernambuco launched a major management reform program. Pernambuco sits on the country's northeastern coast, stretching between its capital of Recife and beautiful beaches to picturesque inland mountains. But the governor believed a determined focus on achieving better results for citizens could transform Pernambuco and its economy. He developed an aggressive system to link goals with performance measurement, with a tight loop connecting what worked back to the budgeting process. His efforts brought policy planning into a single framework, along with substantial input from citizens.[15]

The performance framework produced truly impressive results. In its first eight years, the performance of students improved from 21st to 4th place in Brazil. The school dropout rate improved from almost the worst to the best in the country. Violent crime fell 27 percent. The percentage of homes with public water supply increased from 81 percent to 89 percent; deaths from preventable causes dropped by 9 percent. Eduardo Campos, who launched the reforms, became the most popular governor in Brazil. He went from winning 34 percent of the first-round vote in 2006 to 83 percent in 2010. His successor, Paulo Câmara, continued the reforms – and enjoyed similar political success.[16]

The conventional wisdom is that citizens don't reward good government performance. But Pernambuco's case shows that strong, effective reforms, focused squarely on engaging citizens in the process and producing results that matter to them, can not only produce better government performance. Such reforms can also lead to substantial political success.

Other Latin American cases reinforce the message about the universality of the trust problem and the potential of retail-level reforms for attacking it. In 2003, a professor from the University of the Andes mounted a successful campaign for mayor of Medellín, Colombia, which had long been troubled as the home of one of the world's most powerful drug cartels. As a distinctly unconventional politician, wearing jeans and long hair, Sergio Fajardo made a powerful mark on the drug-war-torn city through an aggressive construction program. Innovative architecture replaced slums where violence once raged. Crime dropped dramatically while spending on education rose, a plan that one observer said was the "strategy he used to kill three birds with one stone" – inequality, violence, and corruption. He focused on government reform by opening government up to scrutiny, through a strategy he called "many eyes, few hands" – a large increase in transparency – to ensure "not a single peso is lost." His development strategy focused on a theory he called the "most beautiful for the most poor," with major infrastructure projects and expanded park land devoted squarely to the city's long-neglected underprivileged. While many problems remained, one analyst concluded: "Medellín is a dramatically different city from what it was during Pablo Escobar's reign of terror in the 1990s, socially, economically, and politically – and it's Sergio Fajardo's hard work that contributed to such a transformation." He became one of Colombia's most popular politicians, won election as his state's governor, and positioned himself for a run at higher office.[17]

In the US, Martin O'Malley championed government reform during his two terms as Baltimore's mayor. He introduced an aggressive "CitiStat" performance management system, to identify the most important problems the city faced, to devise strategies to reduce them, and to follow-up relentlessly. In CitiStat's first four years, violent crime fell almost 40 percent, the largest decline of any major city in the country. Citizens could use a telephone call-in system to report everything from potholes to rats, and the city used that system to solve the problems and report back to citizens. Analysts credited the program with $350 million in savings during its first eight years.[18] O'Malley capitalized on CitiStat's success to win two terms as mayor and then two terms as governor of Maryland. It made him an international figure of government reform, all based on improving citizens' experiences with the governments he led.

*Earning retail trust through
the citizens' experience*

In both the US and around the world, government officials have demonstrated that it is indeed possible to improve the citizen experience by focusing on retail-level operations. Of course, improving citizens' experiences is not the same as strengthening trust in those governments, any more than a private company's efforts to improve the customer experience directly lead to improvements in the company's brand. That's the fundamental distinction between retail- and wholesale-level issues. But these cases reinforce two important conclusions: that citizens are alert to the quality of their government's interactions with them; and that improvements to citizens' experiences have produced political success for those who led the efforts. That, in turn, is a reasonable proxy for improved trust. So there's a very strong reason to believe that by improving the way government works – and by focusing on improvements that matter to citizens – government officials can *earn* trust.

Since the 1980s, governments around the world have sought to improve customer service, but often from very different perspectives. The Westminster-style government reforms launched in the United Kingdom, Australia, and New Zealand sought to make government more responsive by ensuring government programs served citizens better. In the US, the "reinventing government" movement promised a "customer-driven government," focused on "meeting the needs of the customer, not the bureaucracy."[19] These movements have converged on a singular focus: governments, and the people who work for them, need to focus their work more on the needs and desires of citizens, not on their own internal procedures and guidelines.

The customer-based approach transformed the way that many government agencies worked. In the US, many state governments paid more attention to improving the process for obtaining drivers' licenses, to cut down waiting time and to make the experience more pleasant. Some states installed kiosks so drivers could conduct their own required emissions tests on vehicles, at any time they preferred, instead of just during the times when the office was open. At the federal level, the IRS created a website for taxpayers to download tax forms and check to see when tax refunds would be processed. Other governments created one-stop Internet portals, like www.gov.uk, to allow citizens to find the information they needed without having first to guess which agency housed it. Reformers argued that a stronger focus on improving citizens' experience could even make work better for government's employees, because "doing great work is a lot less strain on your people than doing crummy work."[20]

Over the years, however, the customer-experience movement in government has sometimes been attacked, especially by academics arguing that that citizens are not customers, in the private-sector sense. The critics saw the customer service movement as a fundamental violation of the notion of public law, in which government employees had an obligation to administer the law, delegated by policy makers from the top down, instead of treating citizens from the demand side, from the bottom up. The core of the argument was that bottom-up responsiveness, in a retail sense, could confound top-down accountability, from a wholesale direction. Critics did not so much argue against making government more responsive to citizens as for ensuring it was more accountable to policy makers. But as the relationship between governments and their citizens soured, as trust declined, as budgetary pressures increased, and as technology multiplied, most of these criticisms melted away. It became increasingly difficult to argue, moreover, that making paying taxes or getting a driver's license more pleasant was not, in itself, a good thing.

Many governments across the globe have developed substantial customer service plans, focused primarily on putting citizens' needs, not the

interests of government bureaucracies, at the center.
They concluded that, too often in the past, government had focused narrowly on its internal processes
and forced citizens to bend to its rules, rather than
structure those processes to meet citizens' needs. It
was little wonder, they concluded, that citizens felt
disconnected from – and increasingly distrustful of
– a government that seemed uncaring and remote.
Indeed, low levels of service to citizens and higher
levels of distrust seem linked.[21] In putting citizens
at the center, governments have used a broad collection of strategies: streamlining the transactions
that citizens make with government, from airport
security screening to paying taxes; setting ambitious
customer service standards, especially for those
areas where citizens interact most with government;
and more effective use of technology, to make it
easier for citizens to connect with government, on
their terms, exploring what they need and when
they need it. The Obama administration in the US
made customer service one of its top cross-agency
priority goals. In the United Kingdom, the government promised that its website would produce
simpler, clearer, faster service. The government of
Singapore made its customer service program a
global model. Moreover, the IRS's work in the US
demonstrates that a positive customer experience

doesn't rely simply on government agencies providing services that citizens want. If interactions are important and inescapable, citizens clearly appreciate an improved experience, even in paying taxes. That strategy, reformers hoped, might help reverse the "democratic deficit" that plagues so many countries.[22]

The focus on the customer experience has great strength, for several reasons. First, it seems self-evidently the right thing to do. Treating citizens (and taxpayers) better is something that many reformers simply believe is important, in its own right. Second, better service is something citizens increasingly expect. The more they encounter improved service in the private sector, the more they rightly expect it from their government. It's not a world in which government can simply assume it can stay even. Private companies are in a fierce race with each other, and governments will fall farther behind if they don't work hard to keep up. Third, better service can save taxpayer dollars, by reducing duplication and making it easier for government to provide what citizens need. Fourth, at the very least, better customer service is likely to prevent citizens' trust in government from getting worse. Fifth, the evidence from the private sector is that retail-level interactions – improving the customer experience – are far more important for generating sales – and, therefore, profits – than broad brand identity. That is, retail-level forces are likely to be much more important than wholesale-level ones for strengthening citizen confidence.

Earning retail trust through retail-level transparency

There is, moreover, intriguing support for the proposition that stronger retail-level transparency can earn trust. Researchers in Boston conducted two projects in partnership with the city government. In one study, the researchers showed 554 interview subjects a 5-minute video showing city government workers doing their jobs, ranging from building roads to ensuring food safety. The videos demonstrated government workers doing their jobs well. Trust in and support for government services increased. Then the researchers devised a separate experiment, involving 21,786 citizens who used a mobile phone application to request a city service. Some citizens were shown photos of city workers responding to their individual requests, and they were much more likely to continue using the app over the next 13 months. Often, the researchers argued, government's work tends to be "submerged," out of sight from most citizens. Their work, they concluded, showed that "operational transparency led to sustained engagement with government."[23]

Hopeful road

The quest for earning trust is a difficult one indeed. It is very hard for elected officials, during the time they have in office and with the tools they have at their disposal, to make much progress at the wholesale level, especially with the broad problem of income inequality. Increasing transparency is an obvious tactic, but that sometimes can make things worse.

This is a case, however, where the shibboleth of running government more like the private sector makes sense. Where corporate efforts to transform their brands, at the wholesale level, have often fallen short, many companies have made big progress by improving their customers' experience at the retail level. In government, there's powerful evidence that smart leaders have been able to do the same. Can government earn our trust? The answer, from retail-level strategies, is yes.

But this is not easy, in part because it is not yet fully part of government's toolkit – and in part because, as we shall see in the next chapter, there are often substantial barriers to the retail strategy. There is hope for earning trust, therefore, but success ultimately depends on navigating past these hurdles.

4

Blocking Trust

It's certainly possible to earn trust, even in governments where the levels of citizen distrust are high. The barriers to doing so, however, are sometimes deep and wide. Earning trust is expensive. It requires a change in bureaucratic culture as well as in basic processes, to make government's work more citizen-centered: to accommodate bureaucracies to citizens' needs, instead of the other way around. And it works best at the retail-level interactions where, in the spirit of Bagehot, government can truly earn trust. New technologies, such as connecting citizens' online requests with photos of their problems being solved, are neither cheap nor easy. New technologies can be cheap in comparison with transforming bureaucratic cultures. But if government's leaders care about trust, they need to earn it, to invest what it takes, and to lead to ensure it happens.

That, in turn, requires a careful, sustained effort to break the barriers to earning trust.

Barriers to earning trust

Earning trust requires breaking through three barriers: *populism*, the rising struggles of some groups of citizens in society to shrink government's size and break the power of what they perceive to be a ruling class; *proxies*, government's increasing reliance on nongovernmental agents to deliver public services; and *pros*, the public's increasing skepticism about the role of experts, whose guidance paradoxically is needed to devise trust-earning strategies. Retail-level efforts to earn trust have great promise, but the promise will prove hard to keep if these three wholesale-level barriers persist.

Populism

Until the mid-2010s, many analysts had confidently predicted that the world was well on its way to a truly globalized integration of economies and social norms. Barriers to trade were lowering and consumers were enjoying a host of products and services that globalization made possible, from smart phones to easy international travel. But on the heels of the 2008 economic meltdown, a fierce anti-government populism emerged and, in two very different – and two very close – elections in 2016, it unexpectedly transformed politics. At the beginning of 2016, the smart money said that Donald Trump had little chance of being the Republican party's nominee for president, and that Britons were very likely to vote to remain in the European Union. By the end of the year, Trump was planning his move to the White House and a new British prime minister was struggling to manage the country's exit from its historic union with Europe. The rise of this populist movement not only shook political foundations but also created a sharp fissure in how citizens connected with their governments. This double shock built on the broad wholesale-level distrust of governments. That distrust in turn made it far harder for government officials, at the retail level, to earn the trust of their citizens.

According to exit polls in the American presidential election, 23 percent of all voters said they were angry at Washington, and Donald Trump got 77 percent of their votes.[1] In Great Britain, Euroskeptics drove the Leave campaign. Two-thirds of those surveyed before the June vote said that at least some European Union powers ought to be returned to the

British national government. "Favorable" views
about the EU fell from 54 percent of Britons in
2004 to 44 percent in 2016. But there was a sharp
ideological split on the issue. Those on the left were
far more likely to have a favorable opinion about
the EU than those on the right (by a margin of 69
to 38 percent). The biggest driver of negative views
toward the EU was disapproval of how the EU
handled the refugee issue (70 percent) and the
economy (55 percent).[2]

A new populism drove these campaigns, and
those who voted for Trump and for Brexit tended
to be angrier, older, whiter, less-educated, and more
rural.[3] The new populist movement, moreover,
spilled over into non-English-speaking countries. In
Hungary, 98 percent of voters rejected mandatory
EU immigrant quotas in a 2016 referendum, and
populism surged in France, Italy, Greece, and
Austria. Even the once-invincible Chancellor Angela
Merkel saw her support erode, as more Germans
worried that the influx of Muslim refugees threat-
ened the country's economic and social fabric.

These populist movements had tangled roots: a
sense that globalization had helped some groups
but left others behind; that immigrants were robbing
citizens of economic opportunity; that terrorism
posed new, unpredictable threats to citizens' daily

lives; and that many families had been left behind despite a growing economy. Income inequality proved the foundation of populism, just as it was the foundation of populism. In the US, for example, economic growth affected workers very differently. From 1980 to 2014, weekly wages for the top 10 percent of full-time workers rose 38.1 percent, after accounting for inflation. For the bottom 10 percent, however, weekly wages managed just a 1.3 percent gain (see figure 4.1). It is little surprise, moreover, that the two countries where populism reared its head most strongly – the US and Great Britain – ranked as the world's leaders in income inequality (see figure 4.2). Amidst the grand strategies, moreover, there were important social and cultural fissures. Outside analysts often mocked the Trump campaign for running on little more than the candidate's instinct, but his analysts used sophisticated data analytics to identify which issues, like trade and immigration, mattered most to which voters; where campaign rallies were likely to prove most effective, and which themes ought to drive which events; and even which television shows pro-Trump voters were most likely to watch. (Trump's data analytics team, for example, discovered that the television show NCIS, short for "Naval Criminal Investigative Service," was especially popular with

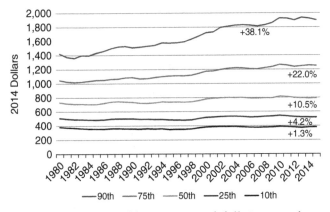

Figure 4.1 US: weekly earnings of full-time workers aged 16 and older, by percentile

Source: U.S. Bureau of Labor Statistics

those who opposed the Obama administration's health-care program.[4])

The modern world had not treated those at the bottom of the income scale kindly and it was little surprise that, as Aspen Institute President Walter Isaacson put it, "resistance to modernity" had become such a major force.[5] Populism rose as trust declined, and distrust proved greatest where inequality was highest.

The contrast of the populist movement of the 2010s with a previous populist movement, at the dawn of the industrial age, is striking. The story of the late nineteenth century is very complex, of

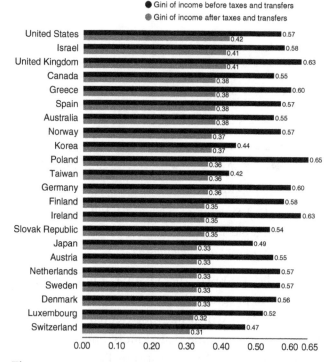

Figure 4.2 Income inequality: before and after taxes and transfers

Data   source: www.ourworldindata.org/data/growth-and-dis tribution-of-prosperity/income-inequality, Luxembourg Income Study (US), and https://goo.gl/8nH16Q.

course, but a signature element of the transition from agrarian to industrial times was the remarkable growth in government's power – and confidence in government's ability to use it well. Along the way, there were fierce battles about the direction of these reforms and about just how strong government's role in society ought to be. However, across the sweep of a generation, in most of the world's major democracies, there was a host of progressive reforms, from the growth of health care and regulation of economic trusts to the spread of women's suffrage and the rise of public investment in education. Moreover, the movement aimed squarely at reducing income inequality. The industrial age created great opportunity for workers. With modest training, often on-the-job, farmers could move into factory jobs that significantly improved their standard of living, and those improvements created broad support for the populist cause. The road, of course, was bumpy and progress was erratic. Working conditions in many factories were dreadful, and violent workers' strikes punctuated the industrial age's growth. But over time, trade unions helped to improve working conditions, government took on a far larger role in managing the economy, and expanding public programs created a large welfare state. Despite the enormous political conflicts along the way, the transformation built strong demand for and great confidence in government's ability to do the job. At the core was confidence that the economic transformation would improve citizens' lives, that it created opportunity for citizens across the board, and that citizens could trust a stronger government to steer the change.

In the transformation that globalization brought, however, the story was very different. Because the transformation built on a shift from heavy manufacturing to information and service jobs, it advantaged those with the education to move into the globalized economy. That hit many middle-class workers – especially middle-aged middle-class workers – particularly hard. Some of their jobs disappeared. Others were shipped abroad as manufacturing became more globalized. Without enough of the right kind of education, these workers often found themselves left behind. Many individuals celebrated the change, and more education created vast new opportunities for a new generation of workers. That proved little consolation, however, for those who didn't have the needed skills and found themselves too late in life to acquire them. Those whom globalization left behind became increasingly angry at government's inability to ensure that the rising tide lifted *their* boats.

The Trump and Brexit campaigns at first seemed like novelties, but it became increasingly clear that they built on deep and fundamental schisms between those that globalization advantaged and those it left behind. Those schisms, moreover, are likely to endure as long as the underlying inequalities remain. Income inequality, of course, has long driven political distrust, but globalization has widened the inequality gap and made it harder to close. For workers making the transformation from the agrarian world to the industrial age, the barriers were far lower than for those coping with the transformation from the industrial age to the information/globalization age. For middle-aged factory workers whose jobs have either disappeared or moved abroad, and where emerging jobs require education the workers simply don't have, the prospects are especially bleak.

Indeed, education has become more important than ever, not only for improving individuals' job prospects but also for shaping their views about government. As Cambridge professor of politics David Runciman argued, "how people vote is increasingly being shaped by how long they spent at school." Trump's success with less-educated white voters mirrored the Brexit vote, and reflected the anti-intellectual tenor of the Brexit campaign. In Britain,

73 percent of those who left school without qualifications voted to Leave. In the US, 67 percent of whites without a college degree backed Trump (see figure 4.3).[6] It seems increasingly likely that their anger will spill over into distrust of government and its commitment to care for them. Education, along with class, age, and race, thus could well become a filter for trust, creating confidence in government for those with more education, whose opportunities are enhanced through globalization, and feeding distrust for those whose lives are not. Populism thus captures a broad collection of issues likely to affect the challenges of earning trust throughout the extended transformation to the information age.

So, at the wholesale level, the prospects for regaining trust lie in government's investment in education, because better education is the route to providing workers with the skills they need for the information age. It's also the foundation for more effective democracy. Thomas Jefferson, one of America's most thoughtful founders, wrote: "I know no safe depository of the ultimate powers of the society but the people themselves; and if we think them not enlightened enough to exercise their control with a wholesome discretion, the remedy is not to take it from them, but to inform their discretion by education. This is the true corrective of

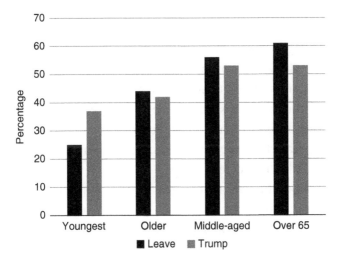

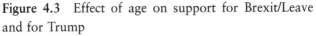

Figure 4.3 Effect of age on support for Brexit/Leave and for Trump

Source: For Trump data: "Election 2016: Exit Polls," *New York Times* (November 8, 2016), www.nytimes.com/interactive/2016/11/08/us/politics/election-exit-polls.html?_r=0. Legend: Youngest – voters aged 18–24, Older – 30–44, Middle-aged – 45–64, and Over 65. For Brexit data: "YouGov Survey Results" (June 23, 2016), http://d25d2506sfb94s.cloudfront.net/cumulus_uploads/document/640yx5m0rx/On_the_Day_FINAL_poll_forwebsite.pdf. Legend: Youngest – 18–24, Older – 25–49, Middle-aged – 50–64, and Over 65.

abuses of constitutional power."[7] He would certainly recognize the fundamental issues of trust facing governance in the twenty-first century. And it's likely that the passing years would have made his commitment to education as "the true corrective of abuses of constitutional power" even greater. He and Bagehot would both also recognize the fundamental challenges to democracy's dignity that the populist movement raises.

Does this mean that retail-level approaches to earning trust are meaningless? Absolutely not. But it does mean that populism builds even barriers to the retail-level strategies and tactics we explored in the last chapter. At the same time, however, the retail strategies for earning trust are real and effective. The higher the wholesale-level barriers of income inequality, the more promise that retail strategies offer: to stem the tide of rising distrust and, if only on the margin, make modest progress in earning citizens' trust.

Proxies

A second major challenge to citizens' connections to government came with the vast expansion of government's interweaving with the private and nongovernmental sectors, especially in the US. It's an intricate puzzle: building retail-level trust is the most effective strategy for earning trust; earning retail-level trust depends on improving citizens' experiences with government; but the more that for-profit and nongovernmental contractors, instead of government's own workers, are the ones who connect with citizens in delivering public services, the harder it is for *government* to earn trust, because it's harder for citizens to see their government at work. The more public programs depend on such a vast and complex network, the harder it is to separate out what is truly *governmental* from what is not.

Citizens increasingly expect that government will solve almost any problem that matters, from preventing their smart phones from bursting into flames to ensuring that the shrimp they buy at the supermarket is safe. Virtually *any* problem can quickly become a *public* problem demanding a governmental response. Indeed, most news stories about big issues increasingly have a tag line, "why didn't government prevent this from happening?" At the same time, especially in the US, government's connections with citizens in attacking problems have become ever more indirect, as more nongovernmental intermediaries have come between citizens and their government. That has vastly complicated the problem of earning trust: creating confidence that government will solve problems, and recognizing when government does it.

Governments, of course, have always relied on contractors to supply goods and services. The Romans, for example, used contractors to construct public buildings hundreds of years before the beginning of the common era. But the use of third parties expanded significantly in the twentieth century to support the great armies that waged world war. As the movement from the right to shrink the size and scope of government grew in the 1980s, some nations sold off major government operations, like the airline and oil company in Great Britain and telecommunications and banking in New Zealand. The US, which had few state-owned enterprises to begin with, contracted out much of government's support work, from the operation of cafeterias to building maintenance and vehicle repair. From the left came pressure to make government more responsive by putting more operational responsibility in neighborhood hands, through community-based organizations, churches, and similar nongovernmental operations. The result was a major transformation of the delivery of government programs, a movement I've called "government by proxy."[8]

Despite very different pressures from the right and the left, the movement has had a singular focus: replacing service delivery by government agencies with nongovernmental entities that, reformers believed, would be more efficient, effective, responsive, and trustworthy. The movement has created one of the most fundamental transformations of governmental strategies and tactics of the modern era. That's been especially the case in the US, but even in countries where the state is large and where government officials have traditionally done all of government's work, the proxy movement is spreading. In Denmark, for example, the government has hired nongovernment guards to supplement local police, to provide additional protection for areas that might be terrorist targets. In China, the government is experimenting with faith-based organizations to provide care for its aging population. The core of the effort is the reliance on *nongovernmental* organizations to support the provision of *governmental* services.

There are raging debates about whether the movement has reduced the size of government or made it more efficient. But one thing is clear: despite its efforts to connect government's operations more closely to the people, the movement hasn't improved trust.

The proxy movement might well connect the front-line delivery of government programs more directly with citizens. But it doesn't connect citizens more directly with government. In fact, as the chain of implementation became longer and more complex, it became much harder for citizens to see government's role clearly in their lives and, therefore, to know whether to trust it more. If a government-funded neighborhood center provides services for senior citizens or day care for children, citizens might like and appreciate it, but they are unlikely to see government's hands in the work. Intricate implementation partnerships can erase the line of sight between citizens and their government.[9] That, in turn, directly challenges the evidence of the Harvard researchers that transparency, both in government's operations and in the connections between government services and citizens, could support the trust-earning process.

In the US, there was a famous campaign sign carried by a woman demanding "keep government's hands off my Medicare," the federal government's program funding health care for the elderly and one of the government's largest programs. Analysts often told the story as an outrageous example of citizen ignorance. In fact, though, there would be no particular reason for the woman to connect the federal government with the health care she received. Federal tax dollars paid for it, but she received the care through a network of for-profit and nonprofit health-care providers. Through government by proxy, she benefited from a huge government program without directly encountering the government. She liked the program and wanted to defend it. She just didn't know – or care – that it was the federal government that was responsible for it. And there was no case for why she ought to trust the government more.

Most nations don't share the US's vastly complicated administrative structure, but the movement toward proxies, both for-profit companies and nongovernmental organizations, is growing around the globe. In this movement, the government rarely gets credit for successes because citizens rarely see government's hand. However, the government often gets blamed for unmet needs. Lower-level governments have an easier time establishing the line of sight with citizens, and that could help explain the higher levels of trust they tend to enjoy. Central governments, however, face far larger challenges in earning trust, the more they rely on nongovernmental partners.

Pros

A third major challenge to the public's trust in government is cynicism about professionals and experts. Of course, there's nothing truly new here. Walter Bagehot said in the mid nineteenth century, "No real English gentleman, in his secret soul, was ever sorry for the death of a political economist."[10] But with rising distrust of government has also come a new wave of suspicion about the role of experts. Indeed, as the growing complexity of society has forced government to rely more on experts, the more the public distrusts them.

Globalized government, in fact, has grown on the backs of policy analysts producing more insights into what, they argue, works best. In the United Kingdom, there's been an important movement devoted to discovering "value for money." In the US, the movement has focused on benefit–cost analysis, randomized controlled trials, and performance management. New Zealand's government grew such confidence in its own expertise that the government developed a new company, "G2G

Know-How," devoted to selling government-developed expertise to other governments. All these approaches build on the fundamental premise that citizens ought to trust experts, because experts can figure out answers for citizens that they can't discover for themselves. And, of course, the more complex that government and the society in which it rests might be, the more citizens need experts. Building rockets and designing airliners are skills beyond what most citizens could master. Air traffic control is an intricate minuet. So too are satellite communication, management of the power grid, and bank-teller machines. Ensuring food safety and homeland security, very different issues, both require great skill. It would be impossible for government to do what citizens expect without the government's reliance on experts.

Experts are essential, but as they have become more important they have become trapped in the fundamental problems of distrust plaguing many institutions. As the populist movement swelled, experts have been caught up in it. In the Brexit battle, Leave supporters were often at a loss to find any expert who supported their position, but they turned that into an asset in their appeals to voters. As one pro-Leave Labour Member of Parliament put it, "There is only one expert that matters, and that's you, the voter."[11] Leave leader Michael Gove famously said that "the British people have had enough of experts."[12]

In fact, a poll just before the vote showed that Britons had little trust in anyone: trust in Prime Minister David Cameron was just 19 percent. Others fared little better: former Prime Minister Tony Blair (12 percent); pro-Leave politicians Nigel Farage (26 percent) and Boris Johnson (39 percent); actors Benedict Cumberbatch (18 percent) and Eddie Izzard (23 percent); think tanks (28 percent); economists (38 percent); political leaders from other countries, like Barack Obama who came to London to make a pitch (14 percent); British politicians (13 percent); journalists and sports figures (both 10 percent); and senior religious figures (15 percent).[13] After the vote, a professor from the Department of Government at the University of Essex concluded, "academic experts are no longer seen as authoritative."[14] The same seems true for just about everyone else. In the US, a quarter of those surveyed in a 2016 poll distrusted the federal government's economic data, including consumer spending and the unemployment trends. Among Trump supporters, the number was twice as high.[15] Not only is distrust of experts rising, but there are deep divisions *among* citizens in distrust. Citizens from the right distrust experts far more, and are more likely to believe things that are not true. Trump voters were far more likely to believe that Obama was born in Kenya, that millions of illegal votes were cast in the 2016 presidential election, and that vaccines cause autism. Distrust plagued those on the left as well, with supporters of Hillary Clinton far more likely to believe that Russia tampered with vote counting in the 2016 election to help Trump.[16]

The problem spread to news coverage, with individuals not trusting the news coverage they were getting and with social media creating echo chambers among people who share opinions – and sometimes "fake news." Fake news has asserted that the pope endorsed a candidate in the 2016 American presidential election and that terrorists funded 20 percent of Hillary Clinton's presidential campaign. One fake news story asserted that a Washington pizza shop was in fact the headquarters for a child sex ring, and that led a North Carolina man to drive north with an assault weapon to investigate. (There was, of course, no child sex ring – just customers and pizza shop workers terrified by his gun.) During the 2016 presidential campaign, fake news received more attention than real news. The top 20 fake-news stories on Facebook were shared 8.7 million times, compared with the 7.4 million shares from the top real-news websites.[17] False stories kept armies of fact-checkers busy – but 88 percent of Trump supporters believed that the news media skewed the facts to support reporters' biases. On the other hand, 59 percent of Clinton supporters trusted the fact-checkers.[18] But it's hard to tell how much any of this matters, since many citizens simply don't trust polls to begin with.[19]

The early days of the Trump presidency only fueled the "fake news" debate. The president tended to label news stories with which he disagreed as "fake" and tweeted that "any negative polls are fake news," implying that the only real polls were those showing support for him.[20] When confronted in an interview about falsehoods uttered by the president in the administration's opening weeks, presidential counselor Kellyanne Conway replied, "Are they more important than the many things that he says that are true that are making a differ-ence in people's lives?"[21] The Trump team finely honed an art of undermining opponents by claiming that what they said couldn't be trusted.

Faced with a hurricane of noise and unimagina-ble complexity, and peering through ideological lenses that distort the view, many citizens simply trust their own common sense over expert opinion. Two-thirds of Leave supporters, in contrast to one-fourth of Remain supporters, said it was wrong to rely on experts – and that it was better to rely on ordinary people. Deeply suspicious of experts and others trying to interpret or shape reality on their behalf, populists have come to distrust specialists and policy mavens.

Rather than enhancing democracy by helping it look farther down the road, experts have become a focus of distrust in themselves. There's a sense that experts have become even more distanced from the real problems of people, perhaps seasoned with a taste of arrogance. The rise of populism, journalist Sebastian Mallaby argued, shattered "the cult of the expert" and experts "will have to demonstrate the skill to earn the public trust, and preserve it by deserving it."[22] Rather than strengthening trust by improving the way government works, experts have become wrapped in the pressures pulling trust down.

The lesson is this. It is indeed possible to earn trust, especially by improving the way government connects with citizens at the retail level. But, even as some officials have developed retail strategies to earn trust, large wholesale-level forces are making that job far more difficult. As we've seen, distrust is deeply rooted in all human interactions, especially in governments. All governments have always had to deal with problems of distrust, and no government has managed to permanently earn trust. Some citizens trust their leaders more than others. But trust in government is breaking down along big fault lines: globalization, income inequality, age, education, and especially ideology. These fault lines have become harder to bridge, and political distrust is but one of the consequences. One of the biggest casualties, in fact, is deep damage to what Bagehot called the "dignity" of government. He wrote about how government could build on the "reverence of the population." There's little more talk of that in the era of political distrust than there are reminders of government's role in "the pursuit of happiness," from America's Declaration of Independence.

In *Richard III*, Gloucester brooded, "Now is the winter of our discontent." Had Gloucester – and Shakespeare – read 21st-century public opinion polls, their discontent might not have been limited to wintertime. Trust in many (but not all) governments is low and getting worse. It's also rooted deeply in big problems entangled around the core of democracy and the relationships between citizens and their governments. In the countries where distrust is rising, the story isn't a happy one. And even in nations like Great Britain, where trust is higher than in the US, political distrust and fears about the average Briton's economic opportunities casts a heavy shadow over confidence in democratic rule.

At some level, of course, facts are facts. There is a time at which astronomers know the sun will rise tomorrow morning. There is the number of people working for the government, the number of contractors assisting them, the amount of money the government spends on a project, and the number of citizens they serve. These facts have never been sovereign. They have never determined what government did, how people perceived what government did, or how much they trusted what government did. But, until recently, the government could declare baseline facts and people would accept them as the foundation of policy debates. American public intellectual and US Senator Daniel Patrick Moynihan famously said, "Everyone is entitled to his own opinion, but not his own facts." But that maxim eroded in the face of the rising tide of populism. There was a growing sense that individuals *were* entitled to their own facts and that, in tandem, facts asserted by others, including by government, couldn't be trusted. Indeed, Trump counselor Kellyanne Conway asserted she would provide "alternative facts" to the facts that the news media had established as true.[23]

To be sure, some facts are squishy, because of the assumptions that analysts must make in acquiring them. In the US, for example, the federal Bureau of Labor Statistics reports unemployment numbers on a monthly, quarterly, and annual basis, with adjustments made along the way to improve accuracy. It produces six different measures of unemployment, based on how long individuals have been out of work, whether they are actively looking or discouraged, and whether they've just completed temporary jobs, among other factors. Economists believe that the different measures provide subtle understanding of the labor market. Cynics believe that they provide the government with many ways to cook the books. To insiders, the numbers seem sophisticated. To outsiders, they can seem slippery. As distrust has grown, that slipperiness in turn has fed distrust of facts. The erosion of an acceptance of core facts – or, even, that there are such things – has not only increased distrust. It's made it harder to have basic public debate about policy.

Downward ratchet

On the bright side, it's worth remembering that trust is neither static nor linear. The evidence is that trust varies over time, that it depends on citizens' sense of whether government is looking out for their interests, and that it grows when their experience with government is positive and when they look to government in times of great crisis. Trust is both cause and effect: trustworthy actions increase trust, and higher levels of trust improve government's work.

But the last generation has also brought a dark side: government seems stuck on a downward ratchet of political distrust. Government rarely benefits from good performance, but it gets the blame for troubles, glitches, and sometimes for larger economic and social forces out of its control. The forces pushing trust in government downwards are stronger and more long-lasting than those pushing it up, and that increasingly makes it hard to recover. For example, strong economic growth, like that in the late 1990s, barely moved the trust needle. Big crises, like the 2001 terrorist attacks in the US, boosted trust, but the increase proved short-lived. On the other hand, sluggish economic growth and rising income inequality pushed trust down, and economic crises drove it down even more.[24]

Thus, the downward drift in political trust proves stickier than advances upward. It could be that a generally distrustful public is cynical about improvements and more likely to focus on problems than successes. It could be that the public believes that government is captured by interests that don't represent them and, therefore, things they disagree with are more likely to occur. It could be that, because of the public's distrust of institutions, it's less likely to give government credit for good things that happen. In general, downward drifts in trust tend to stick; upward improvements tend not to last.

Indeed, that's precisely the evidence from the rating of American presidents. Consider George W. Bush, whose approval rating soared to 90 percent after the 2001 terrorist attacks, a level unmatched by any president after World War II and approached only briefly by Harry Truman (at 87 percent, on taking office), George H.W. Bush (89 percent, at the conclusion of the first Iraq war), and John Kennedy (at 83 percent, soon after taking office). But George W. Bush's approval sank below 50 percent after the federal government's failed response to Hurricane Katrina in 2005, and ultimately sank to 25 percent in 2008, shortly before he left office. The 2001 terrorist attacks and Hurricane Katrina (2005), in fact, were the pivotal moments of his presidency, at least in terms of citizens' approval. The upswing of support following the terrorist attacks on

September 11 didn't stick; the decline following Katrina did.[25]

Barack Obama faced a similar challenge. He came into office with an approval rating of 68 percent. His approval and disapproval ratings were about equal, until the troubled launch of his signature health-care program in 2013. After that, his approval ratings dropped sharply, to 41 percent just a few weeks later. With great struggle, he managed to nudge his approval rating back above 50 percent in the early spring of 2016. In contrast to the turbulent presidential campaign that year, he began looking much better to voters, and his approval ratings rose back above 50 percent.[26] In a bit of bipartisan irony, in fact, Obama's approval numbers tumbled much as Bush's did, at a very similar point in his eight-year term. The difference was that he managed to climb modestly back into positive territory.

In other countries, leaders have likewise found themselves entangled in distrust following policy crises. After the Brexit vote, David Cameron was ranked among the three worst prime ministers of modern times. One of Europe's most popular and durable political figures, German Chancellor Angela Merkel, saw her popularity drop 12 points in a mid-2016 poll, following terror attacks in the country.[27] The problems have tended to cascade into what some observers have called a "legitimation crisis" for government.[28]

The pattern is similar in major democracies: trust in government and, especially, in its leaders tends to be a one-way street. Elected officials often begin with a reservoir of hope and trust. Good news tends to buoy them and crises build support. But these forces are short-lived. Bad news tends to drag down the approval of leaders and trust in their governments and, once lost, support proves hard to recover. Some of this stems from the cause–effect dilemma of political distrust – does distrust weaken political leaders, or do political leaders weaken trust – which is hard for elected officials to untangle and even harder for them to manage. Some of this comes from the inescapable pressures that elected officials face, with ever more complex policy problems, relatively few policy leaders within their direct control, and a very short time frame in which to act.

And some of this flows from the inherent cynicism baked into modern democracies. Bad news travels farther and faster than good news. People seem more inclined to believe negative stories than good ones, at least about government. They don't believe government works well, even when confronted with manifest evidence in their daily lives of high governmental performance, from fires extinguished, accident victims rescued, airline passengers delivered safely by air-traffic control systems, social welfare payments made, and drivers sped to their destinations on good roads. Little is new about the propensity of people to complain. As Benjamin Franklin pointed out, "Any fool can criticize, condemn and complain – and most fools do." In fact, government has always seemed to have two prominent purposes: to solve those problems that citizens collectively seek to solve, and then to provide a focus for their complaints. The ancient Romans no sooner created their government than citizens began complaining about it.[29] That's scarcely surprising when an essential element of government is coercion, and coercion is then used to extract taxes.

Distrust and government are inextricably linked, now as they have been for millennia and will likely be for all time. For millennia, governments have managed to work, often very effectively, despite the overhang of distrust. Any careful look at science fiction, in books and in the movies, hints that humankind in the future will continue to limp along with governments that no one fully trusts. But it's impossible to escape the fact that political distrust has gotten worse, that the downward ratchet is especially pernicious and hard to escape, and that this has proven particularly damaging to democratic government.

Trust and the future of democracy

Earning trust is thus an exceptionally difficult quest. Government officials have important leverage over the economy, but they can't control its cycles. They can try to lead their governments well, but they can't avoid crises. They can create more transparency, but they can't expect that citizens will see translucence to increase trust. They can bring in more experts, but sometimes experts only worsen distrust. And they can try new administrative strategies, but the efforts sometimes disconnect citizens from government itself. They can advance new retail-level strategies to improve the citizen experience, but they still face wholesale-level challenges. And with all these efforts, there's a perverse mismatch: downside pressures tend to stick, while upside gains prove ephemeral.

Distrust isn't a universal phenomenon across governments, but it is a big problem in many – and no government is immune from its constant, lurking presence. Worries about the legitimacy of government and, especially, confidence in its exercise of power unquestionably soar when trust falls. It's often a depressing tale.

But that brings us back to the foundations of the problem.[30] Success at the retail level, in both the public and private sectors, provides clear evidence that it's possible for governments to earn trust by improving their interactions with citizens at the wholesale level, and to make those transactions more transparent to citizens, even though transparency itself is so slippery. At the wholesale level, more and better education of citizens offers additional hope. More-educated citizens are more likely to understand and trust the complexities of their governments. And, since distrust is connected so deeply to income inequality, more and better education is the best tool to help citizens thrive in a rapidly changing – and inextricably global – economy. The best jobs will go to those who can most easily adapt to rapid change. Nations with the best education tend to have the strongest economic growth. Nations with a broader base of high-quality education for all their citizens are more likely to reduce inequality.[31] And less inequality is more likely to feed the fundamental conditions for increasing trust at the wholesale level. It is that combination – a reflection of Bagehot's reminder of the importance of both dignity and effectiveness in government – that offers real promise for earning trust in government. However, he would doubtless be worried about how much the erosion of trust has eaten away at government's dignity.

This is hardly a magic wand to sweep away the distrust that afflicts so many governments. The roots are deep. Many of the driving forces at the wholesale level are powerful, and many lie beyond what individual government leaders can influence at all, let alone during their terms of office. But there's a powerful – and positive – case that government officials can improve government's standing by treating their citizens in trust-earning ways. Those retail strategies might work only at the margins of what otherwise are powerful wholesale forces, but the strategies are real. They are within the control of individual government leaders. They seem to be effective. They can earn trust. And that, in turn, offers the strongest hope for the resilience of democracy in a globalized world.

Afterword: Cynthia of the Desert

Consider this personal tale. In the early 1990s, I served on a task force to advise the US Secretary of Energy. Our focus was on an especially difficult public policy puzzle: where to store the nuclear waste accumulated through the nation's nuclear weapons program and from its nuclear power plants. It's an especially tough problem because a storage facility has to be secure for 10,000 years, longer than the recorded history of life on earth. And it involves some of the nastiest stuff on earth – exposure to even small amounts of radioactive waste can prove dangerous, even fatal – so no one wants a storage facility anywhere near them. Our mission was not to recommend where such a facility ought to go but, rather, how the government could earn the trust of citizens in making that decision.

Can Governments Earn Our Trust?

We traveled extensively and talked with many citizens. Tensions were often very high. We held one public hearing in Las Vegas, not far from one of the proposed storage sites. During the hearing, a woman came up to the microphone and said, "My name is Cynthia of the Desert, and I live in the desert with my husband and child." Members of the advisory committee looked at each other, not sure what was coming next. "I'm concerned with the plan to put waste in the mountain," she continued, "and I don't really trust the government to make the right decision. But I've had long talks with some of the Department of Energy (DOE) scientists working on the problem. They've explained to me what they're doing and how their plans to store the waste will work. I might not trust the government, but I do trust them," she concluded. DOE officials had earned her trust, by working at the retail level, to improve her experience, the lives of the members of her family, and the broader efforts to deal with an important problem from which they couldn't simply walk away.

Notes

1 The Puzzle of Trust

1 Richard Edelman, "A Crisis of Trust: A Warning to Both Business and Government," Edelman Trust Barometer (November 2, 2015), www.theworldin .com/article/10508/crisis-trust?fsrc=scn%2Ffb%2Fte %2Fbl%2Fed%2Ftheworldin2016; Edelman Trust Barometer, "2016 Executive Summary" (2016), www.edelman.com/insights/intellectual-property/ 2016-edelman-trust-barometer/executive-summary; and Public Policy Polling, "Congress Somewhere Below Cockroaches, Traffic Jams, and Nickelback in Americans' Esteem" (January 8, 2013), www .publicpolicypolling.com/main/2013/01/congress- somewhere-below-cockroaches-traffic-jams-and- nickleback-in-americans-esteem.html.

2 There is a wide variety of definitions of "trust," but most converge on the definition used in this book. For a look at the contributions of scholars to this debate, see Kenneth Newton and Pippa Norris,

"*Confidence in Public Institutions: Faith, Culture or Performance?*" (Cambridge, Mass.: Kennedy School of Government, Harvard University, 1999), https://www.hks.harvard.edu/fs/pnorris/Acrobat/NEWTON.PDF; Margaret Levi and Laura Stoker, "Political Trust and Trustworthiness," *Annual Review of Political Science* 3 (2000), 475–507; Marc J. Hetherington, *Why Trust Matters: Declining Political Trust and the Demise of American Liberalism* (Princeton University Press, 2005); Peri K. Blind, "Building Trust in Government in the Twenty-First Century: Review of Literature and Emerging Issues," 7th Global Forum on Reinventing Government (June 26–29, 2007), http://unpan1.un.org/intradoc/groups/public/documents/un/unpan025062.pdf; and Organization for Economic Co-operation and Development (OECD), *Government at a Glance: 2015* (Paris: OECD, 2015), https://goo.gl/5NHM4l.

3 See, for example, Francis Fukuyama, *Trust: The Social Virtues and the Creation of Prosperity* (New York: Free Press, 1995); and Robert D. Putnam, *Bowling Alone: The Collapse and Revival of American Community* (New York: Touchstone, 2000).

4 Gallup, "Americans Still More Trusting in Local Over State Government" (September 19, 2016), www.gallup.com/poll/195656/americans-trusting-local-state-government.aspx.

5 Jennifer Fitzgerald and Jennifer Wolak, "The Roots of Trust in Local Government in Western Europe," *International Political Science Review* 37:1 (2016),

130–46; and OECD, *Government at a Glance: 2013* (Paris: OECD, 2013), p. 34, https://goo.gl/R4g1Uu.

6 OECD, *Government at a Glance: 2013*, p. 33.

7 Pew Research Center, "Beyond Distrust: How Americans View Their Government" (November 23, 2015), www.people-press.org/2015/11/23/beyond-distrust-how-americans-view-their-government.

8 Gallup, "Americans Down on Congress, OK With Own Representative" (May 9, 2013), www.gallup.com/poll/162362/americans-down-congress-own-representative.aspx.

9 Edelman Trust Barometer (2016), slide 15, www.edelman.com/insights/intellectual-property/2016-edelman-trust-barometer/global-results. "Upper-income" individuals are those in the top quartile of income; "lower-income" are those in the bottom quartile.

10 Daniel W. Drezner, "Could the Erosion of Trust in Government Be at an End?" *Washington Post* (September 9, 2016), https://goo.gl/Vt0ybx; and Christopher H. Achen and Larry M. Bartels, *Democracy for Realists: Why Elections Do Not Produce Responsive Government* (Princeton University Press, 2016).

11 An excellent summary of the debate is in Levi and Stoker, "Political Trust and Trustworthiness," pp. 486–91.

12 Amy Fried, "Distrust in Government as a Political Weapon," Scholars Strategy Network (March 2012), https://www.scholarsstrategynetwork.org/sites/default/files/ssn_key_findings_fried_on_distrust_in_government.pdf.

13 Betsy Cooper, Daniel Cox, Rachel Lienesch, and Robert P. Jones, "The Divide Over America's Future: 1950 or 2050?" PRRI (October 25, 2016), www.prri.org/research/divide-americas-future-1950-2050; see also Hannah Fingerhut, "Trump Supporters Far Less Confident than Clinton Backers that Votes Will Be Counted Accurately" (August 19, 2016), www.pewresearch.org/fact-tank/2016/08/19/trump-supporters-far-less-confident-than-clinton-backers-that-votes-will-be-counted-accurately.

14 Kai Ryssdal, "Poll Finds Americans' Economic Anxiety Reaches New High" (October 13, 2016), www.marketplace.org/2016/10/13/economy/americans-economic-anxiety-has-reached-new-high.

15 Richard Edelman, "Brexit and Trust," *Edelman* (June 17, 2016), www.edelman.com/p/6-a-m/brexit-and-trust.

16 Fukuyama, *Trust*, pp. 27–8.

17 OECD, *Government at a Glance: 2013*, ch. 1.

18 Internal Revenue Service, "The Tax Gap: Tax Gap Estimates for Tax Years 2008–2010," https://www.irs.gov/uac/the-tax-gap.

19 Internal Revenue Service, "Federal Tax Compliance Research: Gross and Net Employment Tax Gap Estimates for 1984–1997" (October 1993), p. 11, https://www.irs.gov/pub/irs-soi/p1415e93.pdf.

20 Rasmussen Reports, "Just 31% Trust the IRS" (March 27, 2015), www.rasmussenreports.com/public_content/business/taxes/march_2015/just_31_trust_the_irs.

21 Philippe Aghion, Yann Algan, Pierre Cahuc, and Andrei Shleifer, "Regulation and Distrust," *Quarterly Journal of Economics* 125:3 (August 2010), 1015, 1028.

22 For a broader discussion of the connection between trust and compliance with the law, see Sofie Marien and Marc Hooghie, "Does Political Trust Matter? An Empirical Investigation into the Relation Between Political Trust and Support for Law Compliance," *European Journal of Political Research* 50:2 (March 2011), 267–91.

23 Hetherington, *Why Trust Matters*.

24 OECD, *Government at a Glance: 2013*, ch. 1.

25 Edelman Trust Barometer (2015), www.edelman. com/insights/intellectual-property/2015-edelman-trust-barometer/trust-and-innovation-edelman-trust-barometer; and Nikhil R. Sahni, Maxwell Wessel, and Clayton M. Christensen, "Unleashing Breakthrough Innovation in Government," *Stanford Social Innovation Review* (Summer 2013), https://ssir.org/articles/entry/unleashing_breakthrough_innovation_in_government.

26 Brady Dennis, "'If I could afford to leave, I would.' In Flint, a Water Crisis with No End in Sight," *Washington Post* (October 22, 2016), https://goo.gl/BHTR5y.

27 Donald F. Kettl, *Escaping Jurassic Government: How to Restore America's Lost Commitment to Competence* (Washington: Brookings Institution Press, 2016); Keith Nicholls and J. Steven Picou, "The

Impact of Hurricane Katrina on Trust in Government," *Social Science Quarterly* 94:2 (June 2013), 344–61.

28 "The Death of Trust," *The Economist* (March 10, 2012), www.economist.com/node/21549917.

29 See Marien and Hooghie, "Does Political Trust Matter?"; and OECD, *Government at a Glance: 2013*, p. 21.

30 Rasmussen Reports, "Trump Voters Don't Like the Feds, Clinton Voters Do" (August 29, 2016), www.rasmussenreports.com/public_content/politics/ elections/election_2016/trump_voters_don_t_like_ the_feds_clinton_voters_do.

31 Francis Fukuyama, "The Decay of American Political Institutions," *The American Interest* 9:3 (December 8, 2013), www.the-american-interest.com/2013/12/08/ the-decay-of-american-political-institutions.

32 Simon Longstaff, "Democracy, Trust and Legitimacy," *Papers on Parliament no. 63, Parliament of Australia* (July 2015), www.aph.gov.au/About_ Parliament/Senate/Powers_practice_n_procedures/ pops/pop63/c05.

33 Wikileaks, "HRC Paid Speeches," https://wikileaks .org/podesta-emails/emailid/927.

2 The Case for Distrust

1 "Bible Gateway," https://www.biblegateway.com.

2 King James Version, Matthew 9:11.

3 New American Standard Bible, Luke 19:2.

4 US Department of the Treasury, "History of 'In God We Trust'" (March 8, 2011), https://www.treasury.gov/about/education/Pages/in-god-we-trust.aspx.

5 Jean Shepherd, *In God We Trust: All Others Pay Cash* (Garden City, NY: Doubleday, 1966).

6 John Locke, *Second Treatise on Civil Government*, ch. IV, section 22, www.justiceharvard.org/resources/john-locke-second-treatise-of-government-1690.

7 Ibid., ch. XI, section 136.

8 Ibid., ch. XIX, section 240.

9 See Hetherington, *Why Trust Matters*, p. 67; and Marc J. Hetherington, "The Political Relevance of Political Trust," *American Political Science Review* 92:4 (December 1998), 791–808.

10 American National Election Study, "Trust the Federal Government 1958–2012," http://electionstudies.org/nesguide/toptable/tab5a_1.htm.

11 Pew Research Center, "Public Trust in Government: 1958–2015" (November 23, 2015), www.people-press.org/2015/11/23/public-trust-in-government-1958–2015.

12 Marc J. Hetherington and Thomas J. Rudolph, *Why Washington Won't Work: Polarization, Political Trust, and the Governing Crisis* (University of Chicago Press, 2015), p. 47.

13 Francis Fukuyama, *Political Order and Political Decay: From the Industrial Revolution to the Globalization of Democracy* (New York: Farrar, Straus and Giroux, 2014).

14 Thomas E. Mann and Norman J. Ornstein, *It's Even Worse Than It Looks: How the American*

Constitutional System Collided with the New Politics of Extremism (New York: Basic Books, 2012). See also Hetherington and Rudolph, *Why Washington Won't Work*.

15 Hetherington and Rudolph, *Why Washington Won't Work*, p. 47.

16 Peter H. Schuck, *Why Government Fails So Often: And How It Can Do Better* (Princeton University Press, 2014), p. 4.

17 Gallup, "Restaurants Again Voted Most Popular U.S. Industry" (August 15, 2016), www.gallup.com/poll/194570/restaurants-again-voted-popular-industry.aspx.

18 Barton Swaim, "'Trust, but verify': An Untrustworthy Political Phrase," *Washington Post* (March 11, 2016), https://goo.gl/GTGw7g.

3 Earning Trust

1 Carter Gibson, "You Can't Have Trust Without Transparency," https://community.uservoice.com/blog/you-cant-have-trust-without-transparency.

2 Web Foundation, "Global Rankings" (2015), http://opendatabarometer.org/2ndEdition/analysis/rankings.html.

3 See, for example, a study in Italy by Maria Cucciniello and Greta Nasi, "Transparency for Trust in Government: How Effective is Formal Transparency?" *International Journal of Public Administration* 37:13 (2014), 911–21.

4 Jenny de Fine Licht, "Do We Really Want to Know? The Potentially Negative Effect of Transparency in

Decision Making on Perceived Legitimacy," *Scandinavian Political Studies* 34:3 (2011), 183–201.

5 Stephan Grimmelikhuijsen, Gregory Porumbescu, Boram Hong, and Tobin Im, "The Effect of Transparency on Trust in Government: A Cross-National Comparative Experiment," *Public Administration Review* 73:4 (2013), 573–86.

6 "Trust In America: Recovering What's Lost," *All Things Considered*, National Public Radio (October 30, 2011), www.npr.org/2011/10/30/141844751/trust-in-america-recovering-whats-lost.

7 OECD, "Restoring Trust in Government," www.oecd.org/general/focus/focus-restoring-trust-in-government.htm.

8 See Kate Torgovnick May, "How pervasive has government distrust gotten?" TED Blog (August 13, 2012), http://blog.ted.com/how-pervasive-has-government-distrust-gotten.

9 Walter Bagehot, *The English Constitution* (London: Chapman & Hall, 1867).

10 Putnam, *Bowling Alone*; Fukuyama, *Trust*; Eric M. Uslaner and Mitchell Brown, "Inequality, Trust, and Civic Engagement," *American Politics Research* 31:10 (March 2003), https://www.russellsage.org/sites/all/files/u4/Uslaner%20and%20Brown.pdf; and Hetherington and Rudolph, *Why Washington Won't Work*.

11 Barack Obama, "Remarks by the President on Economic Mobility" (December 4, 2013), https://www.whitehouse.gov/the-press-office/2013/12/04/remarks-president-economic-mobility.

12 See, for example, Jean M. Twenge, W. Keith Campbell, and Nathan T. Carter, "Declines in Trust in Others and Confidence in Institutions among American Adults and Late Adolescents, 1972–2012," *Psychological Science* 25:10 (October 2014), 1914–23; Uslaner and Brown, "Inequality, Trust, and Civic Engagement"; Eric D. Gould and Alexander Hijzen, "Growing Apart, Losing Trust? The Impact of Inequality on Social Capital" (Washington: International Monetary Fund, 2016), https://www.imf.org/external/pubs/ft/wp/2016/wp16176.pdf; and the Edelman Trust Barometer.

13 Forrester, *Expectations vs. Experience: The Good, The Bad, The Opportunity* (June 2016), https://www.accenture.com/t20160825T041338__w__/us-en/_acnmedia/PDF-23/Accenture-Expectations-Vs-Experience-Infographic-June-2016.pdf.

14 Rick Parrish, "The US Federal Customer Experience Index, 2016: Despite Some Bright Spots, Agencies Fail to Meet the Administration's CX Goals," *Forrester* (August 30, 2016).

15 Martin Alessandro, Mariano Lafuente, and Ray Shostak, *Leading from the Center: Pernambuco's Management Model* (Washington: Inter-American Development Bank, 2014), p. 5, https://publications.iadb.org/handle/11319/6435.

16 Edilberto Xavier Jr., "All for Pernambuco Management Model" (Presentation to the Inter-American Development Bank, February 26, 2016).

17 Simon Romero, "Medellín's Nonconformist Mayor Turns Blight to Beauty," *New York Times* (July

15, 2007), www.nytimes.com/2007/07/15/world/
americas/15medellin.html; Saalar Aghili, "Medellín
Rising: Interview with Governor Sergio Fajardo,"
Berkeley Political Review (June 5, 2016), https://
bpr.berkeley.edu/2016/06/05/medellin-rising-
interview-with-governor-sergio-fajardo.

18 Teresita Perez and Reece Rushing, *The CitiStat
Model: How Data-Driven Government Can
Increase Efficiency & Effectiveness* (Washington:
Center for American Progress, April 2007), https://
www.americanprogress.org/wp-content/uploads/
issues/2007/04/pdf/citistat_report.pdf.

19 See Donald F. Kettl, *The Global Public Management Revolution*, 2nd edn. (Washington: Brookings Institution, 2005); and David Osborne and
Ted Gaebler, *Reinventing Government: How the
Entrepreneurial Spirit is Transforming the Public
Sector from Schoolhouse to Statehouse, City Hall
to the Pentagon* (Reading, Mass.: Addison-Wesley,
1992).

20 Micah Solomon, "Why Customer Service Matters,
Even for a Government Agency or Other Sole Provider,"
Forbes (December 7, 2014), www.forbes.com/sites/
micahsolomon/2014/12/07/why-customer-service-
matters-even-in-government-agencies-and-other-
monopolies/#39491f6ee543.

21 Partnership for Public Service, *Government for the
People: The Road to Customer-Centered Services*
(Washington: Partnership for Public Service, 2016),
https://ourpublicservice.org/publications/viewcontent
details.php?id=93.

22 Pippa Norris, *Democratic Deficit: Critical Citizens Revisited* (Cambridge University Press, 2011); and Russell J. Dalton, *Democratic Challenges, Democratic Choices: The Erosion of Political Support in Advanced Industrial Democracies* (Oxford University Press, 2004).

23 Ryan W. Buell, Ethan Porter, and Michael I. Norton, "Surfacing the Submerged State: Operational Transparency Increases Trust in and Engagement with Government." Harvard Business School Working Paper, No. 14-034 (November 2013; revised September 2016), www.hbs.edu/faculty/Pages/item.aspx?num=45842.

4 Blocking Trust

1 William Saletan, "Trump's Voters Don't Support Deportation," Slate.com (November 9, 2016), www.slate.com/articles/news_and_politics/politics/2016/11/debunking_myths_about_trump_voters_with_exit_polls.html.

2 Bruce Stokes, "Euroskepticism Beyond Brexit," Pew Research Center (June 7, 2016), www.pewglobal.org/2016/06/07/euroskepticism-beyond-brexit.

3 "Election 2016: Exit Polls," *New York Times* (November 8, 2016), www.nytimes.com/interactive/2016/11/08/us/politics/election-exit-polls.html; and Arnau Busquets Guardia, "How Brexit Vote Broke Down," *Politico* (June 24, 2016), www.politico.eu/article/graphics-how-the-uk-voted-eu-referendum

-brexit-demographics-age-education-party-london-final-results.

4 Steven Bertoni, "Exclusive Interview: How Jared Kushner Won Trump the White House," *Forbes* (November 2, 2016), www.forbes.com/sites/stevenbertoni/2016/11/22/exclusive-interview-how-jared-kushner-won-trump-the-white-house/#5379bed92f50.

5 Walter Isaacson, on *Charlie Rose* (PBS, broadcast November 10, 2016).

6 David Runciman, "How the Education Gap is Tearing Politics Apart," *The Guardian* (October 5, 2016), https://www.theguardian.com/politics/2016/oct/05/trump-brexit-education-gap-tearing-politics-apart; and Alex Tyson and Shiva Maniam, "Behind Trump's Victory: Divisions by Race, Gender, Education," Pew Research Center (November 9, 2016), www.pewresearch.org/fact-tank/2016/11/09/behind-trumps-victory-divisions-by-race-gender-education.

7 Letter to William Charles Jarvis (September 28, 1820), in Paul Leicester Ford, ed., *The Works of Thomas Jefferson*, vol. XII, *Correspondence and Papers 1816–1826* (New York and London: G. P. Putnam's Sons, 1904–5), https://goo.gl/N8Djbl.

8 Donald F. Kettl, *Government by Proxy: (Mis?)Managing Government Programs* (Washington: CQ Press, 1988). See also Kettl, *Escaping Jurassic Government*.

9 For a discussion of these issues, see Kettl, *Escaping Jurassic Government*.

10 Walter Bagehot, *Frasier's Magazine for Town and Country*, 19 (March 1879), 306. See https://goo.gl/5RineQ.

11 Griff Witte, "9 out of 10 Experts Agree: Britain Doesn't Trust the Experts on Brexit," *Washington Post* (June 21, 2016), https://www.washingtonpost.com/world/europe/9-out-of-10-experts-agree-britain-doesnt-trust-the-experts-on-brexit/2016/06/21/2ccc134a-34a6-11e6-ab9d-1da2b0f24f93_story.html.

12 Michael Deacon, "Michael Gove's Guide to Britain's Greatest Enemy … the Experts," *The Telegraph* (June 10, 2016), www.telegraph.co.uk/news/2016/06/10/michael-goves-guide-to-britains-greatest-enemy-the-experts.

13 YouGov, "Today Programme Survey Results" (June 13–14, 2016), http://d25d2506sfb94s.cloudfront.net/cumulus_uploads/document/x4iynd1mn7/TodayResults_160614_EUReferendum_W.pdf.

14 David Matthews, "Academics Take Stock after Brexiteer Victory over 'the Experts,'" *Times Higher Education* (July 1, 2016), https://www.timeshighereducation.com/academics-take-stock-after-brexiteer-victory-over-the-experts.

15 Ben White and Andrew Hanna, "Depressing Poll of the Day," *Politico* (October 14, 2016), www.politico.com/tipsheets/morning-money/2016/10/depressing-poll-of-the-day-216855.

16 YouGov.US, "Belief in Conspiracies Largely Depends on Political Identity" (December 27, 2016), https://today.yougov.com/news/2016/12/27/belief-conspiracies-largely-depends-political-iden.

17 "Facebook Fake News Performed Better than Real Stories during the Election, According to Report," *Independent* (November 17, 2016), www.independent.co.uk/life-style/gadgets-and-tech/facebook-fake-news-performed-better-than-real-stories-during-the-election-according-to-report-a7422091.html.

18 "Voters Don't Trust Media Fact-Checking," *Rasmussen Reports* (September 30, 2016), www.rasmussenreports.com/public_content/politics/general_politics/september_2016/voters_don_t_trust_media_fact_checking.

19 Ramin Skibba, "The Polling Crisis: How to Tell What People Really Think," *Scientific American* (October 19, 2016), https://www.scientificamerican.com/article/the-polling-crisis-how-to-tell-what-people-really-think.

20 @realDonaldTrump (February 6, 2017).

21 Eli Watkins, "Conway: Do Falsehoods Matter as Much as What We Get Right?" CNN.com (February 7, 2017), www.cnn.com/2017/02/07/politics/kellyanne-conway-donald-trump-falsehoods.

22 Sebastian Mallaby, "The Cult of the Expert – and How It Collapsed," *The Guardian* (October 20, 2016), https://www.theguardian.com/business/2016/oct/20/alan-greenspan-cult-of-expert-and-how-it-collapsed.

23 Alexandra Jaffe, "Kellyanne Conway: WH Spokesman Gave 'Alternative Facts' on Inauguration Crowd," NBCNews.com (January 22, 2017), www.nbcnews.com/politics/politics-news/wh-spokesman-gave-alternative-facts-inauguration-crowd-n710466.

24 Betsey Stevenson and Justin Wolfers, "Trust in Public Institutions over the Business Cycle," National Bureau of Economic Research Working Paper No. 16891 (Cambridge, Mass.: NBER, 2011), www.nber.org/papers/w16891.pdf.

25 Gallup, "Presidential Approval Ratings – Gallup Historical Statistics and Trends," www.gallup.com/poll/116677/presidential-approval-ratings-gallup-historical-statistics-trends.aspx.

26 Gallup, "Gallup Daily: Obama Job Approval," www.gallup.com/poll/113980/gallup-daily-obama-job-approval.aspx.

27 Rainer Buergin, "Merkel's Approval Rating Plunges Following Attacks in Germany," Bloomberg (August 5, 2016), www.bloomberg.com/news/articles/2016-08-05/merkel-s-approval-rating-plunges-following-attacks-in-germany.

28 John Rennie Short, "The 'Legitimation' Crisis in the US: Why Have Americans Lost Trust in Government?" *The Conversation* (October 21, 2016), https://theconversation.com/the-legitimation-crisis-in-the-us-why-have-americans-lost-trust-in-government-67205.

29 Jerry Toner, *Popular Culture in Ancient Rome* (Cambridge: Polity, 2009).

30 The ongoing polls by the Eurobarometer, Gallup, the Pew Research Center, and Edelman, and many country-specific polls around the globe provide rich data to explore. In addition, sophisticated work from scholars provides keen insights. See, in particular, Geert Bouckaert, "Trust and Public Administration,"

Administration 60:1 (2012), 91–115; J. K. Kampen, S. V. De Walle and G. Bouckaert, "Assessing the Relation Between Satisfaction with Public Service Delivery and Trust in Government: The Impact of the Predisposition of Citizens toward Government on Evaluations of its Performance," *Public Performance and Management Review* 29:4 (2006), 387–404; P. K. Blind, "Building Trust in Government in the Twenty-first Century: Review of Literature and Emerging Issues," 7th Global Forum on Reinventing Government: Building Trust in Government (Vienna, 2007); and Putnam, *Bowling Alone*.

31 Ludger Woessmann, "Education Policies to Make Globalization More Inclusive," in Marc Bacchetta and Marion Jansen, eds., *Making Globalization Socially Sustainable* (Geneva: World Trade Organization, 2011), ch. 9, https://www.wto.org/english/res_e/booksp_e/glob_soc_sus_e_chap9_e.pdf.

Further Reading

Understanding the puzzles of trust in government begins with a careful look at public opinion surveys, especially by the Pew Research Center and Gallup. Pew's data file, for example, goes back to 1958. YouGov polling provides useful data on Great Britain, and the Eurobarometer, prepared annually by the European Commission since 1974, contains survey data on the residents of the EU, sorted by the member countries. *Government at a Glance*, issued by the Organization for Economic Co-operation and Development, has very useful data and commentary, and Edelman's Trust Barometer, by the well-regarded public relations firm, contains very useful public- and private-sector comparisons on trust in nations around the world.

Debates about trust in government have deep historic roots. Sources ranging from John Locke's

Second Treatise on Government (1689) to Walter Bagehot's *The English Constitution* (1867) provide invaluable background on the fundamental links between the legitimacy of democratic institutions and trust. The many documents prepared at the time of the American revolution contain especially thoughtful discussions about the nation that its founders were trying to create – and the challenges of legitimacy they believed they needed to solve. The Americans knew they were creating a new country from scratch and wanted to use the best thinking about how to do it. The founding documents, therefore, are rich treasures on the issues of trust and legitimacy.

There is a robust academic literature on trust in government and on related questions of legitimacy and social change, which provide an important background for the issues raised in chapters 1 and 2. Francis Fukuyama's exploration of social trust, *Trust* (New York: Free Press, 1995), is an important base and argues that higher levels of trust promote economic development. He followed that with *Political Order and Political Decay* (New York: Farrar, Straus and Giroux, 2014), which examines how the rise of globalization and interest groups helped to lay the foundation for declining competence in government, which in turn helped to undermine political trust. Robert D. Putnam's provocative *Bowling Alone* (New York: Touchstone, 2000) provides the foundation on which much modern literature on social trust is based.

There is a fascinating analysis of political trust in the political science literature. Among the most useful writings are books by Marc J. Hetherington, including *Why Trust Matters* (Princeton University Press, 2005), and *Why Washington Won't Work* (University of Chicago Press, 2015) with Thomas J. Rudolph. Pippa Norris has developed a rich body of work on "critical citizens," including *Democratic Deficit* (Cambridge University Press, 2011). Russell J. Dalton's *Democratic Challenges, Democratic Choices* (Oxford University Press, 2004) is an invaluable foundation for the debate, as is especially thoughtful research by Geert Bouckaert, particularly "Trust and Public Administration," his 2012 paper in *Administration*. There is also a lively debate on how much citizens' distrust of government builds on government's poor performance. Useful contributions to this debate are Peter H. Schuck's *Why Government Fails So Often* (Princeton University Press, 2014) and Alasdair Roberts's *Can Government Do Anything Right?* (Cambridge: Polity, 2017).

Further Reading

The historical issues in chapter 2, moreover, build on a vast array of classics, from the Bible and the Quran to the writings of the ancient Greeks and Romans, from the philosophers of the Enlightenment to the practitioners who struggled to form the constitutions of new countries like the United States. In fact, one of the most fascinating pieces of the debate about trust in government is not only how this vast array of writings affects how we think about trust, but also how the puzzle of trust provides insight into the fundamental writings on human history.

The debate over wholesale and retail approaches to trust in chapters 3 and 4 builds on the rich practice of many countries. Both the World Bank and the Interamerican Development Bank have produced extensive studies on innovations in countries around the world, especially in Latin America. In the US, the "reinventing government" movement fueled one of the most substantial efforts at ground-up transformation. The book that started it, David Osborne and Ted Gaebler, *Reinventing Government: How the Entrepreneurial Spirit is Transforming the Public Sector from Schoolhouse to Statehouse, City Hall to the Pentagon* (Boston: Addison-Wesley, 1992), remains influential.

At the core of all these arguments is the linkage between citizens and their governments. Do voters decide based on their study of which party is most likely to advance the issues in which they most believe? Or do they vote on the basis of social identities and their partisan loyalties? In a powerful and richly researched book, *Democracy for Realists: Why Elections Do Not Produce Responsive Government* (Princeton University Press, 2016), Christopher H. Achen and Larry M. Bartels persuasively argue that voters rarely vote after careful consideration of the issues but, rather, decide on the basis of groups with which they feel most socially connected. This argument powerfully shapes the background against which the puzzle of trust is set, and the ways in which distrust in government affects the behavior – and indeed the future – of democracy. Trust matters most because it frames the boundaries of governance, as it always has throughout all of human history.